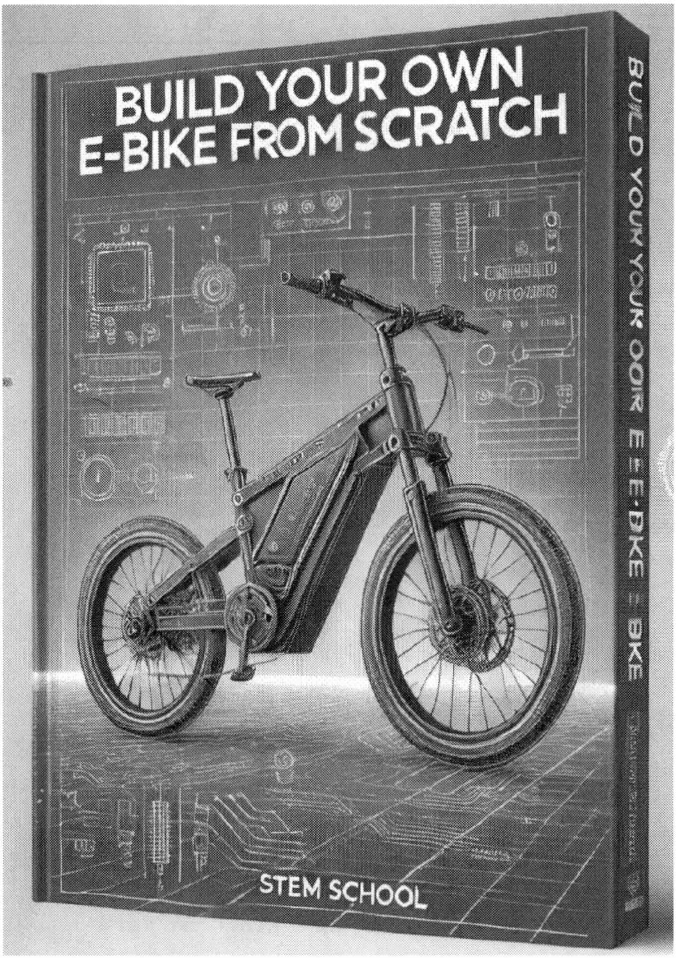
BUILD YOUR OWN
E-BIKE FROM SCRATCH
STEM SCHOOL

Build Your Own E-Bike from Scratch

A Complete Guide for Makers, Engineers and Enthusiasts

By

STEM School

This Page Left Intentionally Blank

Contents

Chapter 1

Introduction to Electric Two-Wheelers

Electric two-wheelers are rapidly transforming the landscape of personal mobility. With advancements in battery technology, motor efficiency, and lightweight materials, electric scooters and motorcycles are becoming viable alternatives to conventional petrol-powered vehicles. This chapter lays the foundation for understanding electric two-wheelers, their advantages, technical components, and the potential for DIY enthusiasts to build their own.

1.1 Understanding Electric Two-Wheelers

An electric two-wheeler is a battery-powered vehicle designed to provide sustainable, cost-effective, and efficient transportation. Unlike traditional fuel-powered motorcycles and scooters, these vehicles rely on electric motors and rechargeable batteries to drive the wheels. This eliminates the need for internal combustion engines, reducing emissions and noise pollution while improving overall efficiency.

Electric two-wheelers come in various forms, ranging from lightweight e-bikes to high-performance electric motorcycles. Their design typically includes a motor (hub or mid-drive), a rechargeable battery, a controller for power management, and electronic throttle and braking systems. Understanding these fundamental components is crucial for anyone looking to build a custom electric two-wheeler from scratch.

1.2 Advantages of Electric Two-Wheelers

One of the main reasons for the increasing popularity of electric two-wheelers is their numerous benefits. These advantages extend beyond just environmental concerns and impact cost savings, performance, and ease of maintenance.

Advantage	Description
Eco-Friendly	Electric two-wheelers produce zero tailpipe emissions, reducing carbon footprint and pollution. Since they do not require fossil fuels, they help decrease dependency on non-renewable energy sources.
Cost Savings	Electric vehicles (EVs) eliminate fuel expenses and have lower operational costs. Maintenance is minimal due to fewer moving parts, reducing long-term expenses.
Efficiency	Electric motors convert more energy into motion compared to internal combustion engines (ICEs). This means greater mileage per unit of energy consumed.
Quiet Operation	Unlike traditional motorcycles, which produce significant noise due to engine combustion and exhaust, electric two-wheelers run almost silently, making them

Advantage	Description
	ideal for urban environments.
Smooth Ride	Electric motors deliver instant torque, providing a seamless and responsive acceleration experience. This makes them more enjoyable to ride, especially in stop-and-go city traffic.
Less Maintenance	With no engine oil, spark plugs, air filters, or complex transmission systems, electric two-wheelers require significantly less upkeep, saving both time and money.

These benefits make electric two-wheelers a compelling alternative for both daily commuters and hobbyists looking to explore new technological possibilities.

1.3 Applications and Market Growth

The adoption of electric two-wheelers is expanding rapidly across various sectors. Governments worldwide are promoting the use of EVs through subsidies and tax benefits, encouraging people to shift toward sustainable transport solutions. The demand for personal electric scooters and motorcycles is rising due to increased awareness of environmental concerns and the need for economical travel options.

Apart from personal commuting, electric two-wheelers are widely used in commercial applications such as last-mile delivery services, ridesharing platforms, and rental fleets. E-commerce companies are increasingly integrating electric delivery bikes into their logistics networks to reduce fuel costs and comply with environmental regulations.

According to recent industry reports, the global electric two-wheeler market is expected to grow at a compound annual growth rate (CAGR) of over 10% in the coming years. This growth is driven by technological advancements in battery energy density, improvements in charging infrastructure, and declining costs of electric vehicle components. With more manufacturers entering the space and governments implementing stricter emissions regulations, the electric two-wheeler industry is poised for continuous expansion.

1.4 Core Technical Components of an Electric Two-Wheeler

To fully understand how electric two-wheelers function, it is essential to break down their core components. Each element plays a vital role in determining the vehicle's performance, efficiency, and overall design.

Battery Technology – The battery is the heart of an electric vehicle, determining its range and performance. Most electric two-wheelers use lithium-ion (Li-ion) or lithium-iron-phosphate (LiFePO4) batteries due to their high energy density and long lifespan. Key factors such as voltage, capacity, and battery management systems (BMS) are crucial considerations in designing an efficient battery pack.

Electric Motor – The motor is responsible for converting electrical energy into mechanical motion. Two main types are commonly used in electric two-wheelers:

> **Hub Motor:** Directly integrated into the wheel, offering simplicity and compact design.
>
> **Mid-Drive Motor:** Positioned at the vehicle's center, connected to the drivetrain for better weight distribution and efficiency.
> Each motor type has its pros and cons, depending on the intended application and performance requirements.

Motor Controller – This component acts as the brain of the electric vehicle, regulating power flow from the battery to the motor. It controls acceleration, regenerative braking, and efficiency optimization, ensuring smooth operation and safety.

Throttle System – Electric two-wheelers utilize electronic throttles (either twist grip or thumb throttle) to control speed. These are typically connected to the controller, translating user input into power output.

Braking System – While conventional mechanical brakes (disc or drum) are still used, many electric vehicles also incorporate **regenerative braking** to recover energy during deceleration, improving overall efficiency.

Charging System – A reliable charging system is essential for battery longevity and convenience. Most electric two-wheelers support **standard AC chargers**, while some high-performance models are equipped with **fast-charging capabilities**.

The following diagram illustrates how these components interact in a typical electric two-wheeler setup:

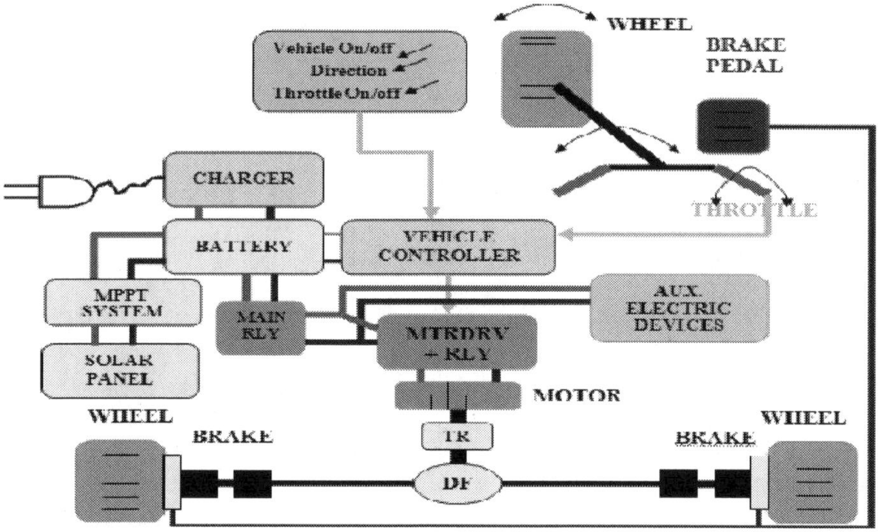

Figure 1 connections between battery, motor, controller, throttle, and braking system

1.5 Why Build Your Own Electric Two-Wheeler?

Building an electric two-wheeler from scratch provides numerous benefits beyond just financial savings. It offers a deeper understanding of electric vehicle technology, allowing enthusiasts to experiment with custom features, optimize performance, and tailor the design to their specific needs. Whether it's modifying an existing bicycle into an e-bike, assembling an electric scooter, or designing a fully customized electric motorcycle, the DIY approach provides complete control over the build process.

Moreover, DIY electric vehicle projects encourage innovation. By learning about motor selection, battery configurations, and controller programming, builders can explore advanced modifications such as regenerative braking, solar charging, or even integrating IoT-based smart features like GPS tracking and mobile app controls.

This book is designed to guide readers through every stage of the DIY process, from selecting components and designing the frame to assembling the vehicle and optimizing performance. The step-by-step approach ensures that even those with minimal prior experience can successfully construct a fully functional electric two-wheeler.

By the end of this book, readers will have the knowledge and confidence to build their own electric vehicle, whether for personal commuting, experimental research, or even as a foundation for launching an EV startup. With growing concerns about fuel costs, environmental impact, and the need for sustainable alternatives, there has never been a better time to explore the world of electric two-wheelers.

Chapter 2

Understanding the Core Components

An electric two-wheeler is an integration of multiple components working together to create an efficient, functional, and reliable mode of transportation. Each component plays a critical role in determining the performance, safety, and longevity of the vehicle. This chapter provides a deep dive into the three most essential elements: the **frame and chassis**, the **electric motor**, and the **battery pack**. A comprehensive understanding of these components is crucial for designing and building a well-balanced and efficient electric two-wheeler.

2.1 Frame & Chassis: The Structural Backbone of the Vehicle

The frame and chassis serve as the foundation of the electric two-wheeler, providing structural integrity and housing essential components such as the battery, motor, controller, and suspension system. The design of the frame affects not only the durability and weight of the vehicle but also its stability, aerodynamics, and ride comfort.

The selection of materials for the frame is crucial, as it directly impacts the strength-to-weight ratio, cost, and ease of fabrication. The most commonly used materials in electric two-wheelers are steel, aluminum, and composite materials.

Comparison of Common Frame Materials

Material	Advantages	Disadvantages
Mild Steel	High strength, cost-effective, easy to weld	Heavy, susceptible to rust
Aluminum	Lightweight, corrosion-resistant, good strength-to-weight ratio	Expensive, requires specialized welding
Carbon Fiber	Extremely lightweight, high tensile strength, corrosion-resistant	Very expensive, difficult to repair
Chromoly Steel	Stronger and lighter than mild steel, good durability	More expensive than mild steel, requires heat treatment

In addition to selecting the right material, the geometry of the frame is a crucial aspect of design. A well-designed frame distributes weight evenly, maintains a low center of gravity, and provides sufficient space for mounting all essential components.

Different types of frames are used in electric two-wheelers, such as **step-through frames** (common in scooters for easy mounting and dismounting) and **cradle frames** (seen in motorcycles for enhanced stability and durability). The frame must also incorporate mounting points for the battery pack and motor, ensuring a secure fit while maintaining accessibility for maintenance.

Fabrication Methods

The construction of the frame typically involves techniques such as **welding, brazing, and CNC machining**. For DIY builders, MIG or TIG welding is commonly used due to its precision and strength. The joints must be properly reinforced, especially at stress points such as the head tube and rear swingarm mounts.

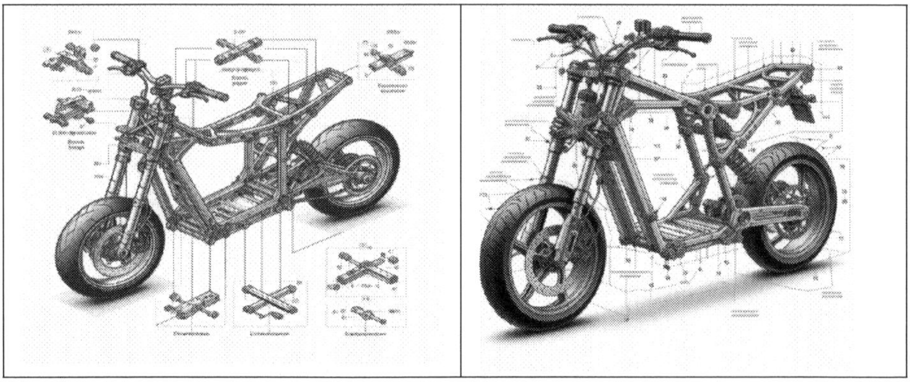

A well-engineered chassis significantly enhances the vehicle's performance by ensuring proper weight distribution, which affects handling, acceleration, and braking efficiency. It is also essential to incorporate **suspension systems** that absorb shocks and improve ride comfort, particularly for off-road or high-speed applications.

2.2 Electric Motor: The Heart of Propulsion

The motor is the primary component responsible for converting electrical energy into mechanical motion. The performance of the electric two-wheeler largely depends on the selection of the right motor type, power rating, torque characteristics, and efficiency.

Two primary types of motors are used in electric two-wheelers: **hub motors** and **mid-drive motors**.

Comparison of Hub Motors and Mid-Drive Motors

Motor Type	**Advantages**	**Disadvantages**
Hub Motor	Simple installation, no need for chains or belts, low maintenance	Heavier unsprung weight, less efficient for steep inclines
Mid-Drive Motor	Better weight distribution, higher efficiency, allows use of bicycle gears	More complex installation, requires a drivetrain, more expensive

Hub motors are **directly integrated into the wheel** and are popular in electric scooters and commuter bikes. They are easier to install, require minimal maintenance, and offer silent operation. However, they add to the **unsprung weight** of the vehicle, which can impact handling and ride quality.

Mid-drive motors, on the other hand, are mounted at the center of the frame and transmit power via a **chain or belt drive**. These motors offer superior performance, especially on **hilly terrains**, as they leverage the vehicle's existing gear system. Mid-drive motors also provide **better weight distribution**, enhancing overall handling.

The power rating of an electric motor is measured in **watts (W)**, and the torque is measured in **Newton-meters (Nm)**. Selecting the appropriate motor involves considering the **desired speed, acceleration, and load capacity**. A motor with **higher torque** ensures better acceleration, especially for heavier loads or uphill rides.

Motor Power Ratings and Performance

Motor Power	**Top Speed (km/h)**	**Torque (Nm)**	**Typical Application**
250W - 500W	25 - 35	10 - 20	Lightweight e-bikes, city scooters
750W - 1000W	40 - 55	20 - 40	Mid-range scooters, cargo e-bikes
1500W - 3000W	60 - 90	40 - 80	High-performance electric motorcycles

Proper motor selection ensures that the vehicle meets performance expectations while optimizing battery efficiency. **Cooling mechanisms**, such as **heat sinks or forced-air cooling**, can be integrated to prevent overheating in high-power motors.

Figure 2 Hub motor vs. a mid-drive motor

2.3 Battery Pack: The Energy Storage System

The battery pack is the most **crucial and expensive** component of an electric two-wheeler, determining its range, power output, and lifespan. The most commonly used battery technologies are **Lithium-Ion (Li-ion)** and **Lead-Acid** batteries.

Comparison of Lithium-Ion vs. Lead-Acid Batteries

Battery Type	**Energy Density (Wh/kg)**	**Lifespan (Charge Cycles)**	**Weight**	**Cost**
Lead-Acid	30 - 50	300 - 500	Heavy	Low
Lithium-Ion	150 - 250	1000 - 3000	Lightweight	Higher

Lithium-ion batteries are preferred due to their **higher energy density, lower weight, and longer lifespan** compared to lead-acid batteries. They also offer **faster charging times** and require minimal maintenance. However, **thermal management** is crucial to prevent overheating and extend battery life.

Battery capacity is measured in **ampere-hours (Ah)** and voltage (V). The total energy storage, expressed in **watt-hours (Wh)**, is calculated as:

Energy (Wh)=Voltage (V)×Capacity (Ah)\ {Energy (Wh)} = \ {Voltage (V)} \times \ {Capacity (Ah)}Energy (Wh)=Voltage (V)×Capacity (Ah)

For example, a **60V 20Ah battery pack** stores **1200Wh of energy**, providing an approximate range of **40-60 km** depending on motor efficiency and terrain conditions.

Battery safety is another critical consideration. A **Battery Management System (BMS)** is required to monitor cell voltage, prevent overcharging, and balance individual cell voltages. Proper **enclosure design** with adequate **cooling** ensures battery longevity and safety.

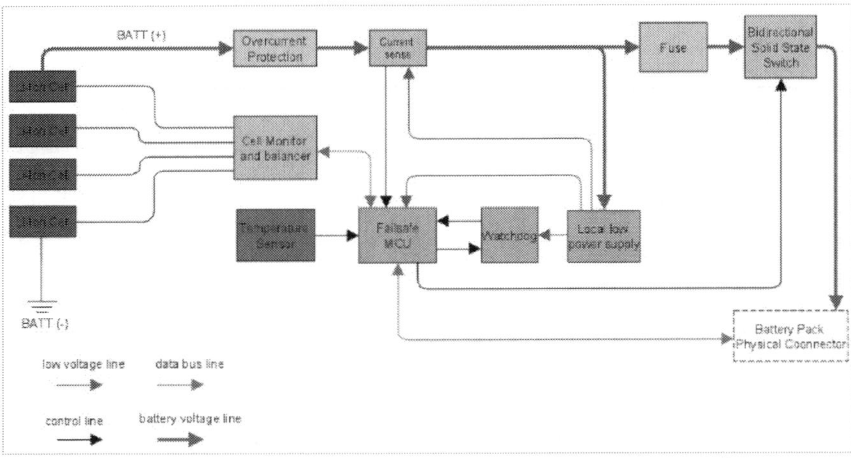

Figure 3 Battery pack wiring and BMS integration

Understanding the Motor Controller

Building an electric two-wheeler requires an in-depth understanding of several key systems that directly impact performance, efficiency, and safety. Among these, the **motor controller**, **throttle and braking systems**, and **wheels, suspension, and tires** play crucial roles. The motor controller regulates the power delivery to the motor, the throttle and braking systems determine acceleration and deceleration behavior, and the choice of wheels, suspension, and tires influences stability and ride quality. This chapter provides a comprehensive explanation of these systems, detailing their functionality, types, advantages, and engineering considerations.

Motor Controller

The motor controller is one of the most critical components of an electric two-wheeler, responsible for **controlling power flow from the battery to the motor**. It acts as the **bridge between the throttle and the motor**, converting user input into precise speed and torque control. The controller ensures smooth acceleration, maintains efficiency, and protects the electrical system from damage due to voltage fluctuations or excessive current draw.

Pulse Width Modulation (PWM) Control

Most electric two-wheelers utilize **Pulse Width Modulation (PWM)** to regulate power delivery. Instead of supplying a constant voltage to the motor, PWM rapidly switches the power on and off at high frequencies, controlling the **average voltage and current** reaching the motor. This results in precise speed control while reducing power loss and heat generation.

The fundamental equation governing PWM duty cycle and output voltage is:

Vout=Vbattery×Duty Cycle(%)100V_{out} = V_{battery} \times \frac{{Duty Cycle} (\%)}{100}Vout

=Vbattery×100Duty Cycle(%)

For example, if a **60V battery** is used and the controller operates at a **50% duty cycle**, the effective voltage supplied to the motor is **30V**. By adjusting the duty cycle, the motor's speed and torque can be efficiently controlled.

Regenerative Braking and Energy Recovery

One of the advanced features of modern motor controllers is **regenerative braking**. Instead of dissipating excess energy as heat during braking, regenerative braking converts kinetic energy back into electrical energy, which is then fed back into the battery. This improves overall efficiency and extends the vehicle's range.

The regenerative braking process involves:

1. The motor switching to generator mode when the rider releases the throttle or applies the brakes.
2. The controller directing the generated electricity to the battery for storage.
3. A controlled deceleration effect, reducing reliance on mechanical braking.

While regenerative braking enhances efficiency, it is most effective at moderate speeds and works best with **brushless DC (BLDC) motors** and **permanent magnet synchronous motors (PMSM)**. A properly configured **Battery Management System (BMS)** is also required to ensure that the recovered energy does not exceed battery voltage limits.

Interfacing with Throttle and Sensors

The controller receives input from various sensors, primarily the **throttle position sensor**, **brake sensors**, and **temperature sensors**.

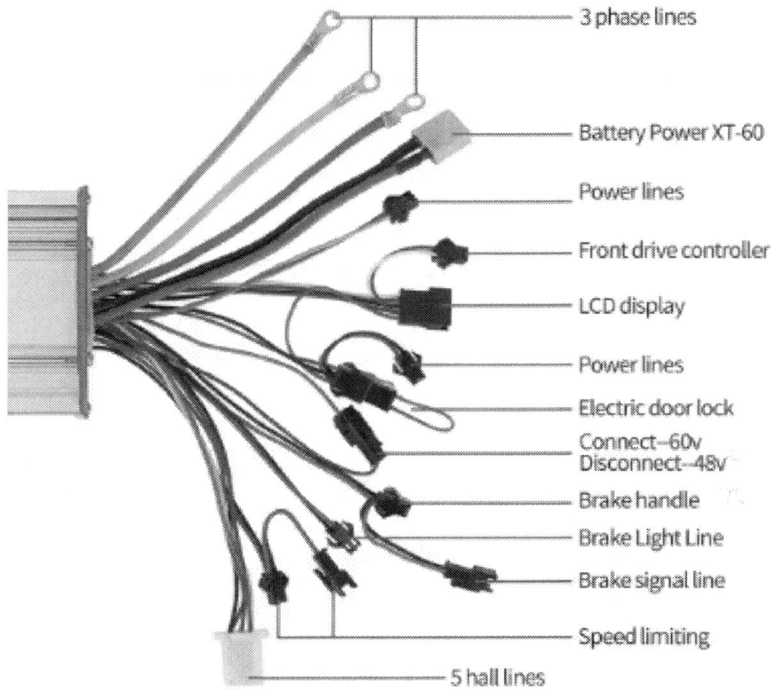

Figure 4 Motor controller connects to the throttle, motor, battery sensors

The throttle provides acceleration commands, while the brake sensors determine when to activate regenerative braking. Temperature sensors prevent overheating by limiting power output when excessive heat is detected.

Throttle & Braking Systems

The throttle and braking systems define how the rider interacts with the electric two-wheeler. A well-designed throttle ensures smooth acceleration, while an efficient braking system guarantees safety and control.

Types of Throttles in Electric Two-Wheelers

The throttle serves as the **primary input device**, allowing riders to control speed. The most common throttle types include **hall-effect twist throttles**, **thumb throttles**, and **pedal-assist sensors (PAS) in electric bicycles**.

Throttle Type	Advantages	Disadvantages
Twist Throttle	Provides intuitive motorcycle-like control, smooth operation	Can cause wrist strain during long rides
Thumb Throttle	Compact, easier to use with one hand	May be uncomfortable for prolonged use
Pedal-Assist Sensor (PAS)	Ideal for hybrid e-bikes, automatically adjusts power based on pedaling force	Less direct control over speed

Most modern throttles use **hall-effect sensors**, which detect the rotation of the throttle and send a voltage signal (typically 0-5V) to the controller. A properly calibrated throttle ensures **progressive acceleration**, preventing sudden jerks that could destabilize the rider.

Braking Systems

A well-designed braking system is crucial for safety, and electric two-wheelers typically utilize a combination of **regenerative braking and mechanical braking**.

Regenerative braking, as discussed earlier, captures kinetic energy and reduces reliance on mechanical braking components, thereby increasing their lifespan. However, regenerative braking alone is insufficient for emergency stops, necessitating **mechanical braking systems** such as **disc brakes** and **drum brakes**.

Brake Type	**Advantages**	**Disadvantages**
Disc Brake (Hydraulic)	High stopping power, effective in all weather conditions	More expensive, requires maintenance
Disc Brake	Affordable, decent	Requires manual adjustments, less

Brake Type	Advantages	Disadvantages
(Mechanical)	stopping power	efficient than hydraulic brakes
Drum Brake	Sealed design prevents dirt ingress, lower maintenance	Less effective cooling, can overheat with prolonged use

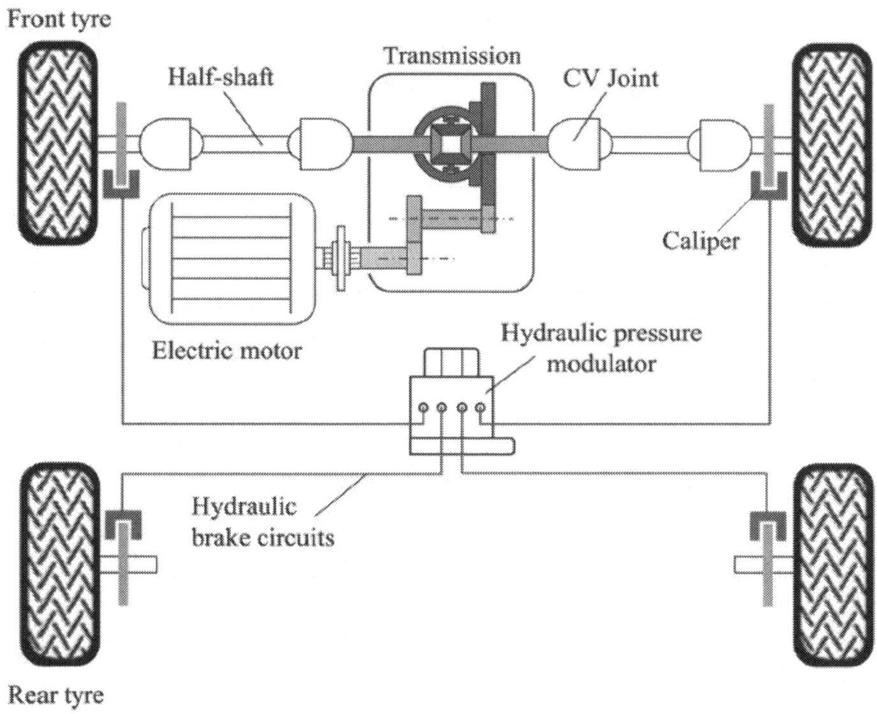

Figure 5 Integration of Regenerative and Mechanical braking

Wheels, Suspension & Tires

The **wheels, suspension, and tires** form the interface between the vehicle and the road, significantly influencing ride comfort, handling, and safety.

Selecting the Right Wheel Size and Material

The choice of wheel size affects the vehicle's acceleration, top speed, and stability. Smaller wheels (10–12 inches) offer **faster acceleration and better maneuverability**, while larger wheels (16–18 inches) provide **higher stability and smoother rides**.

Common Wheel Materials

Wheel Material	**Advantages**	**Disadvantages**
Aluminum Alloy	Lightweight, corrosion-resistant, strong	More expensive
Steel	Strong, durable, cost-effective	Heavier, prone to rust
Magnesium Alloy	Ultra-lightweight, high strength	Expensive, less commonly available

A proper **suspension system** ensures a comfortable ride by absorbing shocks from road imperfections. There are two main types of suspension used in electric two-wheelers:

1. **Telescopic Fork Suspension (Front Suspension)** – Used in motorcycles and scooters, providing excellent shock absorption and ride comfort.
2. **Monoshock or Dual Shock Absorbers (Rear Suspension)** – Helps maintain stability and enhances traction.

A well-balanced suspension system significantly reduces rider fatigue and improves handling, especially on rough terrain.

Choosing the Right Tires for Performance

The choice of tires affects traction, braking efficiency, and ride comfort. Pneumatic tires (air-filled) provide **better shock absorption**, while solid rubber tires eliminate the risk of punctures but offer a rougher ride.

Tire Tread and Performance

Tire Type	Best For	Drawbacks
Knobby Tires	Off-road riding, enhanced grip	Higher rolling resistance, lower

Tire Type	Best For	Drawbacks
		efficiency
Slick Tires	Smooth roads, higher efficiency	Poor grip on wet surfaces
Hybrid Tires	Combination of on-road and off-road use	Moderate efficiency, balanced grip

Figure 6 Wheel size and tire treads on ride comfort

With a thorough understanding of the **motor controller, throttle and braking systems, and wheels, suspension, and tires**, readers will be prepared to optimize their designs for **performance, efficiency, and safety**.

Chapter 3

Material Selection for Building an Electric Two Wheeler

The choice of materials plays a crucial role in the design, performance, and longevity of an electric two-wheeler. Every component, from the frame to the battery enclosure, motor housing, and wiring, must be selected based on its mechanical properties, thermal conductivity, electrical efficiency, and durability. An optimal selection balances **weight, strength, cost, and safety**, ensuring that the final product is efficient, reliable, and capable of withstanding real-world conditions.

Frame Materials

The **frame** is the backbone of any two-wheeler, providing structural support and withstanding mechanical stresses from riding, braking, and impact forces. A well-designed frame must be **strong enough** to handle these loads while remaining **lightweight** for efficiency and maneuverability. The three most common materials used for electric two-wheeler frames are **steel, aluminum, and carbon fiber**, each offering unique benefits and trade-offs.

Material	Density (g/cm^3)	Tensile Strength (MPa)	Weight Considerations	Cost	Durability

Material	Density (g/cm³)	Tensile Strength (MPa)	Weight Considerations	Cost	Durability
Steel (Mild & Alloy Steel)	7.85	250–900	Heavy, but very strong	Low	High
Aluminum Alloy (6061, 7075, etc.)	2.7	200–600	Lighter than steel, good strength	Moderate	Moderate
Carbon Fiber Composite	1.5–2.0	600–1500	Extremely lightweight and strong	High	Can be brittle under impact

Steel is the traditional choice for motorcycle frames, offering high strength, durability, and ease of welding. However, it is significantly heavier than aluminum and carbon fiber, which can reduce efficiency in an electric two-wheeler. Aluminum, particularly **6061 or 7075 alloys**, provides a good balance between weight and strength, making it a preferred choice for **light electric motorcycles and e-bikes**. Carbon fiber offers the best weight-to-strength ratio but is costly and more difficult to repair.

A well-designed **frame geometry**, incorporating **reinforcement points at stress-prone areas**, ensures a longer lifespan and better handling.

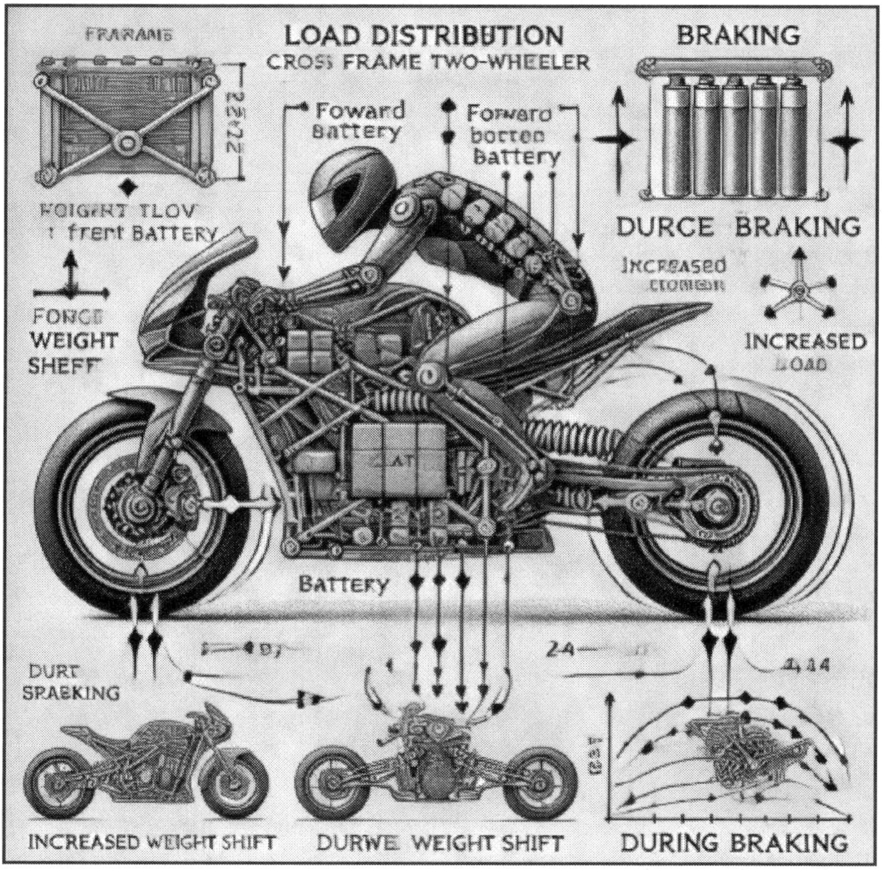

Figure 7 Load distribution across the frame

Battery Enclosure

The **battery enclosure** is one of the most critical safety components in an electric two-wheeler. It must protect the battery cells from **mechanical impact, water ingress, and thermal hazards**, especially given the fire risks associated with **lithium-ion batteries**. Ideal materials for battery enclosures should be:

1. **Fire-resistant** to prevent battery fires from spreading.
2. **Lightweight** to avoid unnecessary weight increase.
3. **Durable and impact-resistant** to protect against crashes or falls.

Common materials used for battery enclosures include:

Material	Fire Resistance	Weight	Impact Resistance	Cost
Aluminum (5052, 6061 alloys)	Excellent	Moderate	High	Medium
Polycarbonate (PC) Plastic	Good	Very Low	Moderate	Low
Fiberglass Reinforced	High	Low	High	Medium

Material	Fire Resistance	Weight	Impact Resistance	Cost
Plastic (FRP)				
Sheet Steel (Galvanized or Stainless)	Excellent	High	Very High	Low

Aluminum is commonly used for **high-performance electric motorcycles** because it is lightweight, corrosion-resistant, and an excellent heat conductor, allowing for passive cooling of the battery pack. **Polycarbonate plastic** is used in some **budget electric scooters**, offering affordability and weight reduction, though it has lower impact resistance. **Fiberglass-reinforced plastic (FRP)** is a strong, non-conductive alternative that provides high impact resistance while remaining relatively lightweight.

For safety, a **thermal insulation layer** may be incorporated into the battery enclosure to prevent thermal runaway.

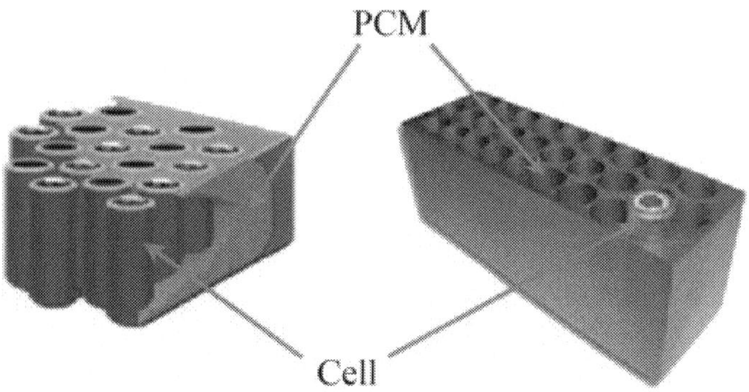

Figure 8 Multi-layer battery housing with fire-resistant insulation

Motor Housing

The **motor housing** protects the **stator, rotor, and internal electronics** from dust, moisture, and mechanical damage while also playing a crucial role in heat dissipation. Since electric motors generate heat during operation, the **material used for the housing** must effectively dissipate this heat to prevent overheating, which can reduce efficiency and lifespan.

Material	Thermal Conductivity (W/m·K)	Weight	Corrosion Resistance	Heat Dissipation Ability
Aluminum Alloy (6061,	150–200	Light	High	Excellent

Material	Thermal Conductivity (W/m·K)	Weight	Corrosion Resistance	Heat Dissipation Ability
7075, etc.)				
Magnesium Alloy	50–100	Very Light	Moderate	Good
Steel	40–60	Heavy	High	Poor
Polymer Composite (ABS, Nylon, etc.)	<1	Very Light	High	Very Poor

Most electric motors, especially **Brushless DC (BLDC) and Permanent Magnet Synchronous Motors (PMSM)**, use **aluminum housings** due to their **high thermal conductivity**, allowing them to dissipate heat quickly. **Magnesium alloys** offer even lower weight but are more prone to corrosion. Steel is occasionally used but is heavier and retains more heat, requiring additional cooling mechanisms. **Polymer composites** are rarely used in high-power motors but can be found in **low-power applications** where heat dissipation is less critical.

Figure 9 Motor Thermal Simulation

Wiring and Connectors: Conductivity, Insulation, and Durability

The **wiring system** in an electric two-wheeler must efficiently carry high currents while ensuring safety and long-term durability. The selection of **conductor materials, insulation types, and connectors** is crucial to prevent **power losses, overheating, and potential short circuits**.

Choosing the Right Conductor Material

Copper and aluminum are the two primary choices for electrical wiring.

Material	**Electrical Conductivity (% IACS)**	**Weight**	**Cost**	**Durability**
Copper (Cu)	100%	Heavy	High	High
Aluminum (Al)	~61%	Light	Low	Moderate

Copper is the **most efficient conductor**, offering **lower resistance and better flexibility**. However, it is heavier and more expensive than aluminum. Aluminum wires are lighter and cheaper but require **thicker gauges** to carry the same current as copper. For high-power electric vehicles, **oxygen-free copper (OFC) cables** are recommended for optimal conductivity and longevity.

Insulation Materials for Wires

The insulation protects against **short circuits, heat, and environmental factors**.

Insulation Material	Temperature Resistance (°C)	Flexibility	Durability
PVC (Polyvinyl Chloride)	80–105	Moderate	Moderate
XLPE (Cross-linked Polyethylene)	125–150	High	Very High
Silicone Rubber	200+	Very High	High

XLPE-insulated wires are ideal for **high-power electric motorcycles**, offering **excellent heat resistance and flexibility**. **Silicone-insulated wires** are used in **racing or high-performance applications** due to their extreme temperature tolerance.

A wiring schematic showing **proper wire routing, gauge selection, and insulation layers** can provide a practical guide for readers.

Material Selection for Wheels, Tires, Suspension

The performance, durability, and riding comfort of an electric two-wheeler depend significantly on the materials used in its **wheels, tires, and suspension system**. These components directly affect the vehicle's handling, efficiency, and overall safety. The selection of materials must balance **cost, weight, performance,**

and longevity, ensuring that the final build provides **stability, road grip, and shock absorption** while remaining affordable and easy to maintain.

Wheel Rims and Tires

The **wheels of an electric two-wheeler** consist of two major components: **the rim and the tire**. The rim provides structural support, while the tire is responsible for grip, shock absorption, and road contact. Both components must be **durable, lightweight, and suited to the vehicle's intended use**, whether for daily commuting, off-road riding, or high-speed performance.

Rim Materials

Two primary types of rims are used in electric two-wheelers: **alloy wheels and spoke wheels**. Each has its own set of advantages and is suitable for different riding conditions.

Type of Rim	Material Used	Weight	Strength	Durability	Best Used For

Type of Rim	**Material Used**	**Weight**	**Strength**	**Durability**	**Best Used For**
Alloy Wheels	Aluminum Alloy, Magnesium Alloy	Lighter	High	Corrosion-resistant	Urban commuting, high-speed riding
Spoke Wheels	Steel, Stainless Steel, Aluminum	Heavier	Very High	Requires maintenance	Off-road, rugged terrains

Alloy wheels are typically **cast or forged aluminum**, sometimes reinforced with magnesium or carbon fiber for **high-performance electric motorcycles**. These wheels provide **better aerodynamics**, are resistant to rust, and require less maintenance compared to spoke wheels. However, they are **more expensive and less shock-absorbent**.

Spoke wheels, made from **steel or aluminum spokes mounted on a central hub**, provide **higher flexibility and shock absorption**, making them ideal for **off-road and adventure electric motorcycles**. They can handle rough terrains well but require **regular maintenance** since the spokes can loosen or bend over time.

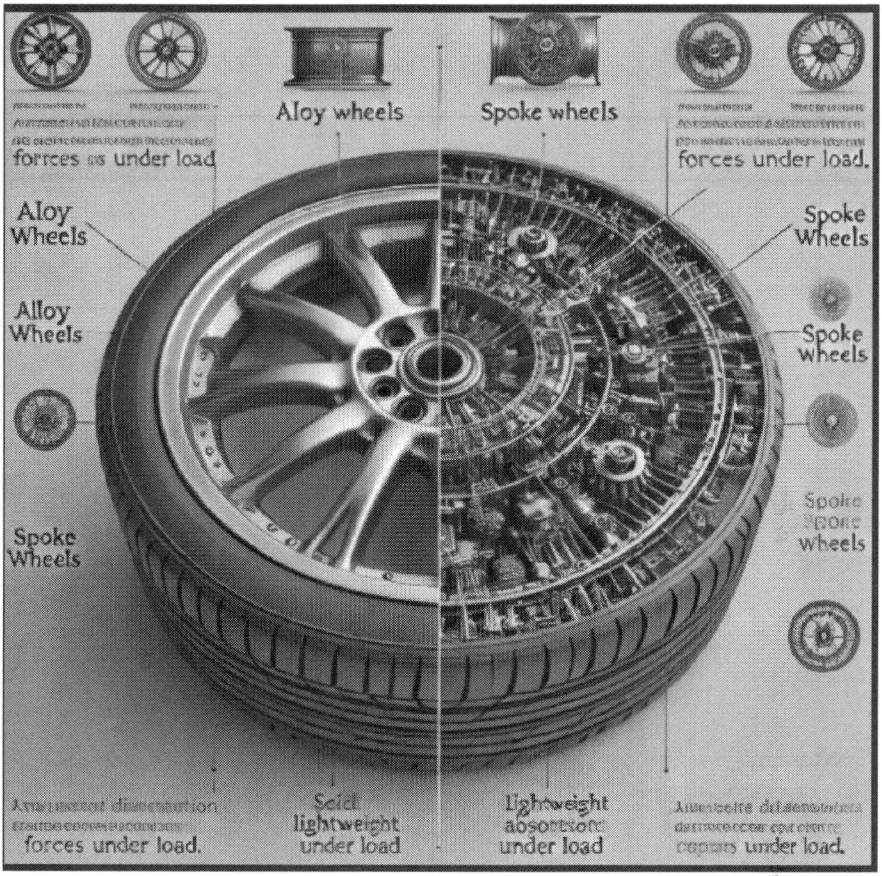

Figure 10 A cross-sectional Wheel Diagram

Tire Materials

Tires are critical for safety, traction, and overall ride comfort. The **rubber compounds used in tires** significantly affect their **grip, wear resistance, and rolling efficiency**.

Tire Type	**Rubber Compound**	**Durability**	**Grip**	**Rolling Resistance**	**Best Used For**
Soft Compound Tires	High natural rubber content	Low	Very High	Moderate	Racing, high-speed riding
Hard Compound Tires	More synthetic rubber	Very High	Moderate	Low	Long-distance commuting
Dual Compound Tires	Combination of soft & hard rubber	High	High	Moderate	All-purpose use

Soft compound tires provide **excellent road grip**, especially in **wet conditions**, but wear out faster. Hard compound tires last longer but may reduce traction, especially on **wet or uneven roads**. Dual-compound tires balance both characteristics, with a **softer rubber on the edges for cornering grip and a harder center for durability**.

For electric two-wheelers, **low rolling resistance tires** are preferred for increasing range and battery efficiency. Some manufacturers also add **silica-based compounds** to improve traction without increasing wear.

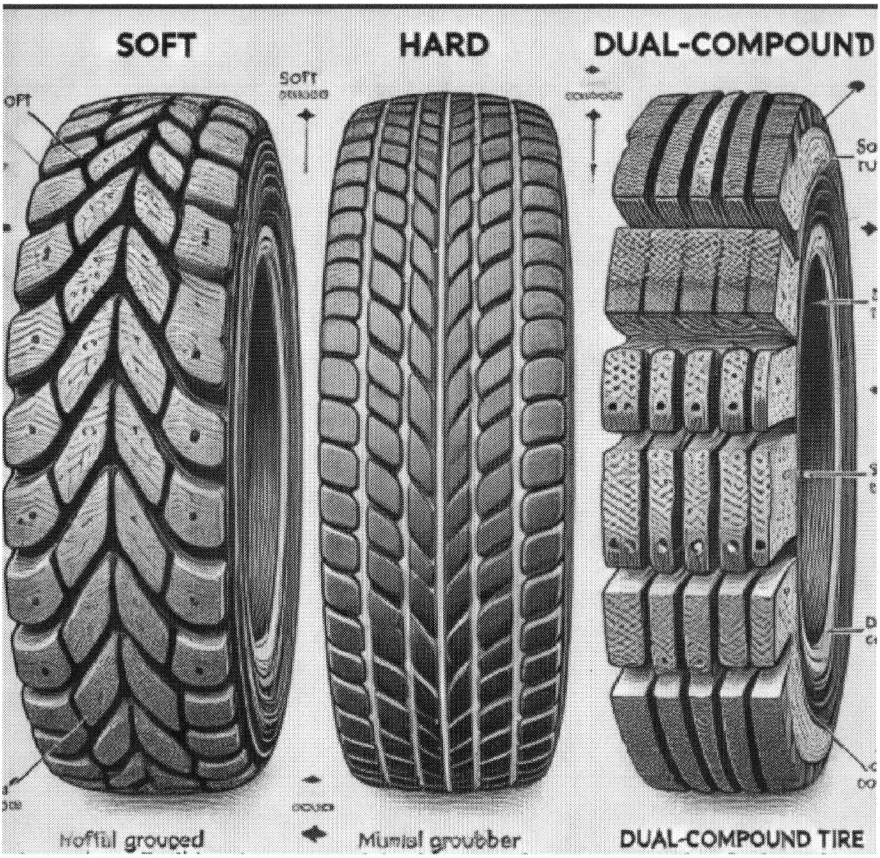

Figure 11 A diagram illustrating the tread patterns of soft, hard, and dual-compound tires

Suspension System: Choosing Materials for Ride Comfort and Durability

The **suspension system** is responsible for absorbing shocks, improving stability, and ensuring a smooth ride. In electric two-wheelers, the two main types of suspension are **telescopic forks (front suspension) and shock absorbers (rear suspension)**. The materials used in these components affect their **performance, weight, and durability**.

Spring Materials

The core component of most suspension systems is the **spring**, which compresses and expands to absorb shocks.

Spring Material	**Weight**	**Durability**	**Corrosion Resistance**	**Cost**	**Best Used For**
Spring Steel (Carbon Steel, Chromium-Vanadium	Heavy	Very High	Low	Moderate	Heavy-duty, high-load vehicles

Spring Material	Weight	Durability	Corrosion Resistance	Cost	Best Used For
Steel)					
High-Strength Polymers (Fiber-reinforced plastics, Composites)	Light	Moderate	High	High	Lightweight electric motorcycles

Traditional **spring steel**, particularly **chromium-vanadium or carbon steel**, is commonly used due to its **high durability and excellent shock absorption capacity**. However, it adds weight to the vehicle and is prone to corrosion if not properly coated.

High-strength polymer-based suspensions are being explored in modern electric motorcycles due to their **lightweight nature and corrosion resistance**. Some advanced polymer springs provide **comparable shock absorption** with a significant weight reduction, enhancing overall energy efficiency.

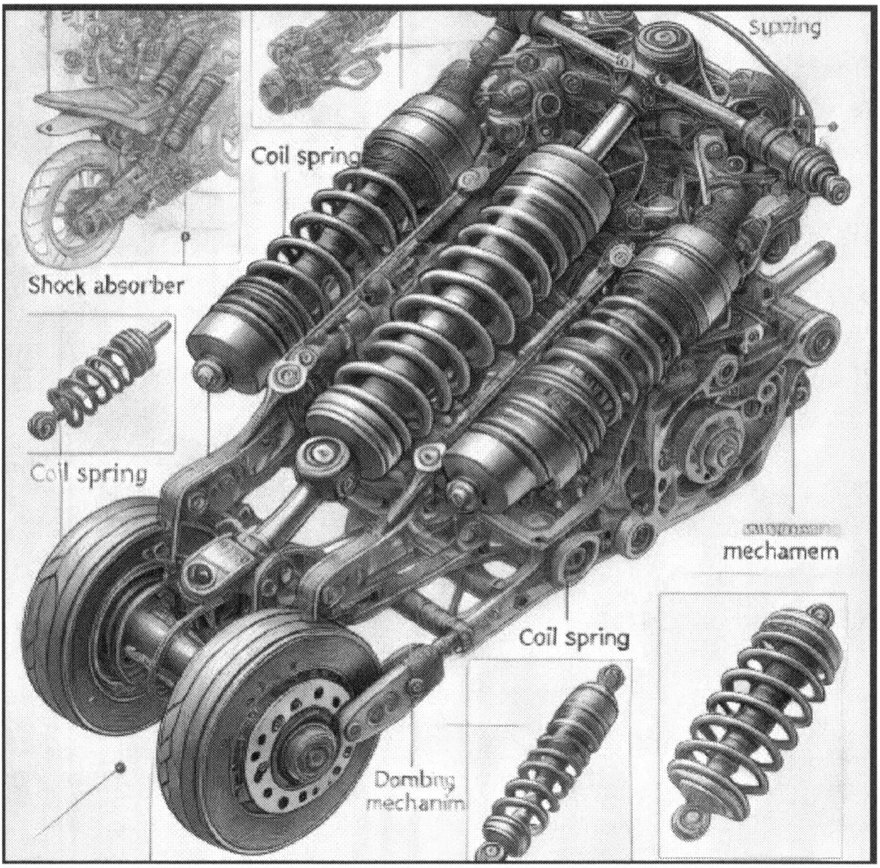

Figure 12 A suspension system

Cost vs. Performance

Building an electric two-wheeler requires making trade-offs between **cost, performance, durability, and efficiency**. Some materials may offer better performance but at a **higher cost**, while others might be **budget-friendly** but require more maintenance or compromise efficiency. Understanding these trade-offs helps in selecting the right materials for a **cost-effective and high-performance build**.

Component	**High-Performance Option (Expensive)**	**Budget Option (Affordable)**
Frame	Carbon Fiber	Steel
Battery Enclosure	Aluminum Alloy	Polycarbonate Plastic
Motor Housing	Magnesium Alloy	Steel
Wheels	Forged Alloy Wheels	Spoke Wheels (Steel)
Tires	Dual-Compound, Low Rolling Resistance	Hard-Compound Rubber
Suspension	Polymer Composite Springs	Spring Steel

For hobbyists and DIY builders working on **cost-effective electric scooters or motorcycles**, materials like **steel, polycarbonate, and spoke wheels** can keep costs low while ensuring reliability. However, for those focusing on **high-performance builds**, lightweight materials such as **carbon fiber, aluminum alloys, and dual-compound tires** provide significant advantages.

A **flowchart guiding users on selecting materials based on their budget and performance priorities** would be an excellent addition to help readers make informed choices.

Balancing Performance, Safety and Cost

The **wheels, tires, and suspension system** of an electric two-wheeler must work in harmony to ensure **stability, safety, and energy efficiency**. The right materials can **enhance acceleration, increase battery range, and improve ride comfort**. Whether opting for **high-end alloys and advanced composites** or sticking with **cost-effective traditional materials**, understanding the characteristics and trade-offs of each choice is essential for a successful build.

With a well-thought-out selection of **lightweight, durable, and cost-efficient materials**, builders can achieve the **perfect balance between affordability and performance**, ensuring their electric two-wheeler meets both functional and aesthetic expectations.

Chapter 4

Designing the Electric Two Wheeler

Designing an electric two-wheeler involves a combination of **aesthetic appeal, mechanical integrity, and electrical efficiency**. The process requires careful planning, starting from initial sketches to detailed 3D models and simulations. Every aspect of the design, from weight distribution to aerodynamics, affects the overall performance and safety of the vehicle. This chapter provides a comprehensive guide to conceptualizing and designing a fully functional electric two-wheeler, ensuring that each component is optimized for efficiency, balance, and real-world usability.

Concept Design: From Sketch to 3D Modeling

The design process begins with **concept sketches**, which help in visualizing the overall shape, size, and structure of the electric two-wheeler. These sketches should consider **ergonomics, aerodynamics, and functionality**. Traditional motorcycles and scooters follow specific design principles, but since electric two-wheelers have different space requirements—mainly for battery placement and motor housing—careful modifications are necessary.

Once the initial sketches are refined, the next step is to create a **3D model using CAD (Computer-Aided Design) software**. CAD modeling is essential as it allows designers to evaluate the dimensions, fitment of components, and structural integrity before physical prototyping.

Popular CAD software options for designing electric two-wheelers include:

Software	**Best For**	**Features**	**Complexity Level**
SolidWorks	Mechanical design, frame modeling	Parametric modeling, stress analysis	Intermediate-High
Fusion 360	3D modeling, electrical integration	Cloud-based collaboration, simulation tools	Intermediate
AutoCAD	2D sketches, initial layout	Precise drafting tools, used for blueprint creation	Beginner-Intermediate
Blender	Concept visualization, rendering	High-quality rendering for design visualization	Beginner-Intermediate
CATIA	Advanced aerodynamics,	Complex surfacing,	High

Software	Best For	Features	Complexity Level
	vehicle body	aerospace-grade accuracy	

A well-designed **3D CAD model** helps in identifying potential design flaws and refining the layout of major components like the **chassis, battery pack, motor placement, and suspension system**.

Figure 13 CAD model

Weight Distribution and Center of Gravity

A critical factor in electric two-wheeler design is **weight distribution**. Unlike traditional motorcycles that primarily house their weight around the fuel tank and engine, electric two-wheelers have **battery packs and motors** that significantly alter the weight distribution.

An **improper weight distribution** can lead to issues such as:

- Poor handling and cornering ability.
- Instability at higher speeds.
- Excessive load on the front or rear suspension.
- Increased risk of tipping over during sudden acceleration or braking.

The **center of gravity (CoG)** plays a vital role in ensuring ride stability. Ideally, the CoG should be as **low as possible and centrally located** to maintain balance. Placing heavy components, like the **battery pack**, near the center of the chassis helps prevent front-heavy or rear-heavy designs.

Component	Ideal Placement for Balance	Effect on Stability
Battery Pack	Low and central within the frame	Lower CoG, improved stability

Component	Ideal Placement for Balance	Effect on Stability
Electric Motor	Mid-mounted for motorcycles, hub-mounted for scooters	Hub motors shift weight to wheels, mid-mounted motors balance the frame
Controller Unit	Under the seat or integrated into the frame	Avoids imbalance, protects from impact
Suspension System	Front telescopic forks, rear mono-shock or dual shocks	Absorbs shocks, improves handling

The table above outlines how different components affect stability and what placement strategies work best.

To further illustrate weight distribution, a **graphical representation of different weight distributions in electric motorcycles vs. conventional motorcycles** would help readers visualize how shifting battery positions affects balance.

Proper weight distribution also impacts **rider comfort**. A poorly balanced vehicle can cause excessive strain on the rider's arms (if front-heavy) or lead to unstable rear wheel traction (if rear-heavy). By fine-tuning the placement of components in CAD software, designers can simulate how different configurations affect the ride quality before finalizing the design.

Load Calculations

Designing an electric two-wheeler requires precise **load calculations** to ensure the vehicle performs optimally under various conditions. The total load on the vehicle includes the **rider's weight, battery pack, motor, chassis, and additional accessories**. Miscalculations in load-bearing capacity can lead to **reduced efficiency, poor handling, and even structural failure**.

The total weight capacity of an electric two-wheeler depends on several factors, including **frame material, suspension type, tire load rating, and powertrain efficiency**. The first step in load estimation is determining the **gross vehicle weight (GVW)**, which includes the weight of all components plus an assumed **maximum rider and cargo weight**.

1. Estimating Gross Vehicle Weight (GVW)

The **GVW** is calculated as:

GVW=(Frame+Motor+Battery+Wheels+Suspension+Controller)+(Rider+Cargo)GVW = (Frame + Motor + Battery + Wheels

+ Suspension + Controller) + (Rider + Cargo)GVW=(Frame+Motor+Battery+Wheels+Suspension+Controller)+(Rider+Cargo)

Assume an average e-bike or electric scooter setup with the following approximate weights:

Component	**Weight (kg)**
Frame (Aluminum)	12-18
Electric Motor (3 kW)	8-12
Battery Pack (48V, 30Ah)	12-18
Wheels & Tires	6-10
Suspension System	5-8
Motor Controller	1.5-3
Total Vehicle Weight	45-65 kg
Rider Weight (Average)	65-80
Cargo or Extra Load	10-15
Gross Vehicle Weight (GVW)	120-160 kg

From this estimation, the **GVW of a typical electric two-wheeler falls between 120-160 kg**. This value is crucial for **suspension tuning, motor selection, and braking system design**.

2. Calculating Power Requirements

The power required to move an electric two-wheeler is influenced by **rolling resistance, aerodynamic drag, gradient climbing ability, and acceleration force**. The total power requirement can be estimated using the equation:

P=F×vP = F \times vP=F×v

where **P** is power (Watts), **F** is the total force required (Newtons), and **v** is velocity (m/s).

The force required to move the vehicle consists of:

1. **Rolling Resistance Force** Fr=Cr×m×gF_r = C_r \times m \times gFr=Cr×m×g
2. **Aerodynamic Drag Force** Fd=12CdρAv2F_d = \frac{1}{2} C_d \rho A v^2Fd=21CdρAv2
3. **Gradient Force** Fg=m×g×sin(θ)F_g = m \times g \times \sin(\theta)Fg=m×g×sin(θ)

Where:

- CrC_rCr = rolling resistance coefficient (0.005–0.015 for bikes)
- CdC_dCd = drag coefficient (0.6–1 for motorcycles)
- ρ\rhoρ = air density (~1.225 kg/m³)

- AAA = frontal area (m²)
- vvv = velocity (m/s)
- mmm = mass of vehicle + rider (kg)
- ggg = 9.81 m/s² (gravity)
- θ\thetaθ = road slope (degrees)

Assuming a 150 kg electric two-wheeler moving at **50 km/h (13.88 m/s) on a flat road**, with **C_r = 0.01** and **C_d = 0.8**, the power required would be:

1. Rolling resistance force: Fr=0.01×150×9.81=14.71NF_r = 0.01 \times 150 \times 9.81 = 14.71 NFr=0.01×150×9.81=14.71N
2. Aerodynamic drag force: Fd=12×0.8×1.225×0.6×(13.88)2=44.2NF_d = \frac{1}{2} \times 0.8 \times 1.225 \times 0.6 \times (13.88)^2 = 44.2 NFd=21×0.8×1.225×0.6×(13.88)2=44.2N
3. Gradient force (flat road, θ=0\theta = 0θ=0): Fg=0F_g = 0Fg=0
4. Total force: F=14.71+44.2=58.91NF = 14.71 + 44.2 = 58.91 NF=14.71+44.2=58.91N
5. Power required: P=58.91×13.88=818.2WP = 58.91 \times 13.88 = 818.2 WP=58.91×13.88=818.2W

Thus, at **50 km/h**, the vehicle requires approximately **820W** just to overcome rolling resistance and aerodynamic drag. To accommodate acceleration and terrain variations, a motor with at least **2-3 times this power (1.5-2.5 kW)** is recommended.

A **graph showing power requirements vs. speed** can help illustrate how much power different speeds demand.

Safety Considerations

Safety is a top priority in electric two-wheeler design. Ensuring structural integrity, proper insulation of electrical components, and compliance with safety standards significantly **reduces risks of mechanical failure, electric shocks, and thermal hazards**.

1. Structural Integrity and Chassis Strength

The **frame and chassis must withstand the dynamic loads** of acceleration, braking, cornering, and uneven road conditions. Testing methods such as **Finite Element Analysis (FEA)** can simulate stresses on the frame under real-world conditions.

Common **frame materials** and their impact on structural integrity:

Material	**Tensile Strength (MPa)**	**Weight (kg/m³)**	**Durability**	**Cost**
Steel (Mild)	400-550	7850	High	Low
Aluminum	250-450	2700	Medium	Medium

Material	Tensile Strength (MPa)	Weight (kg/m^3)	Durability	Cost
Alloy				
Carbon Fiber	600-900	1800	Very High	High

2. Electrical Insulation and Fire Safety

Electric two-wheelers contain **high-voltage battery packs** that require proper insulation to **prevent short circuits, overheating, and fire hazards**. Materials for electrical insulation must have **high dielectric strength** and **thermal resistance**.

Component	Insulation Material	Purpose
Battery Pack Enclosure	**Polycarbonate, ABS, Aluminum**	Fire resistance and mechanical protection
High-Voltage Wiring	**XLPE (Cross-Linked Polyethylene), Teflon**	Prevents electrical leakage and heat damage
Motor	**Varnished Copper,**	Ensures high efficiency and

Component	Insulation Material	Purpose
Windings	**Epoxy-Coated Wire**	longevity

A **table comparing different battery insulation materials** helps in selecting the best option based on **heat resistance, cost, and durability**.

3. Compliance with Safety Standards

Electric two-wheelers must comply with **international and regional safety standards** to be legally roadworthy. Important standards include:

Standard	Regulation Focus	Region
IEC 62133	Battery safety testing	International
ISO 6469	Functional safety of electric vehicles	International
FMVSS 218	Helmet and rider protection	USA
AIS 156	Electric vehicle battery safety	India

Adhering to these standards ensures that the vehicle is **safe for public roads, protects the rider from potential hazards, and meets legal requirements**.

Chapter 5

Building the Chassis and Frame

The chassis and frame of an electric two-wheeler form the **foundation of the entire build**, determining structural integrity, weight distribution, and overall performance. The frame must be **strong enough to support the rider, battery pack, motor, and other components**, while being **lightweight enough** to ensure high efficiency and maneuverability. The design of the chassis also influences **handling, stability, and ride comfort**, making this chapter a critical aspect of the DIY process.

Materials & Tools Required

Selecting the right material for the chassis is essential for ensuring **strength, durability, and weight efficiency**. The most commonly used materials for frame construction include **steel, aluminum, and carbon fiber**, each with its own advantages and trade-offs.

Material	**Strength (MPa)**	**Density (g/cm³)**	**Weight**	**Durability**	**Cost**	**Ease of Fabrication**
Mild Steel	400-550	7.85	Heavy	High	Low	Easy

Material	Strength (MPa)	Density (g/cm³)	Weight	Durability	Cost	Ease of Fabrication
Aluminum Alloy	250-450	2.70	Medium	Medium	Medium	Moderate
Carbon Fiber	600-900	1.80	Very Light	Very High	High	Difficult

For **DIY builders**, mild steel and aluminum are the most practical choices. **Mild steel is easier to weld and more affordable,** while aluminum offers a good balance between weight and strength but requires **TIG welding** for proper assembly.

Tools Required for Frame Fabrication

To fabricate a frame from scratch or modify an existing frame, the following tools are required:

Metal Cutting Tools – A hacksaw, angle grinder, or plasma cutter can be used to cut steel or aluminum tubing.

Welding Equipment – A **MIG or TIG welder** is essential for joining metal tubes securely. **MIG welding** is easier for beginners, whereas **TIG welding** provides better precision, especially for aluminum.

Measuring & Marking Tools – A measuring tape, calipers, and chalk markers ensure accurate cuts and alignments.

Drill & Hole Saws – Used for creating mounting points for the motor, battery pack, and controller.

Jigs & Clamps – Helps hold frame components in position during welding to maintain alignment.

Figure 14 Basic Tools

Step-by-Step Frame Fabrication

There are two approaches to obtaining a frame: **fabricating one from metal tubing** or **modifying an existing bicycle or scooter frame**.

Method 1: Fabricating a Frame from Scratch

Designing the Frame Layout
The first step is to sketch the frame design or create a **3D CAD model** for precise dimensions. Key aspects to consider include:

> **Wheelbase:** The distance between the front and rear wheels should be between **1.2 to 1.5 meters** for stability.
>
> **Head Tube Angle:** A head tube angle of **65-75°** ensures proper steering response.
>
> **Battery and Motor Placement:** Keeping heavy components **low and centered** helps maintain balance.

Cutting the Tubes

Using a **metal cutting saw or grinder**, cut the steel or aluminum tubing according to the frame design. **Ensure accurate cuts** to maintain symmetry.

Welding the Frame

Tack-weld the main sections together first, **checking alignment at each step**. Once the geometry is verified, **fully weld the joints** to maximize strength. A **jig** can be used to hold components in place.

Reinforcing Stress Points

Additional bracing is necessary at **high-stress points**, such as the **head tube (steering area)** and **motor mount section**. Using **gussets and triangular reinforcements** increases durability.

Sanding and Painting

After welding, grind and smoothen all joints. Apply **rust-proof paint or powder coating** to protect the frame from corrosion.

Method 2: Modifying an Existing Bicycle or Scooter Frame

For builders looking for a simpler approach, modifying a **bicycle or old scooter frame** is a viable option.

1. **Stripping the Frame**
   Remove unnecessary components such as the **pedals, fuel tank (if from a scooter), and unnecessary brackets**.
2. **Strengthening the Frame**
   Since bicycle frames are not designed for heavy

motors and batteries, **reinforce weak areas** by welding additional support tubes.

3. **Adding Motor Mounts and Battery Brackets** Weld or bolt **custom brackets** to hold the motor and battery pack securely.

A **comparison between fabricating a new frame and modifying an existing one** can help readers choose the best option for their needs.

Feature	**Fabricating from Scratch**	**Modifying Existing Frame**
Customization	Fully customizable	Limited by original design
Strength & Durability	High	May require reinforcement
Difficulty Level	Advanced	Moderate
Time Required	Longer	Shorter
Cost	Higher	Lower

Mounting Components

Once the frame is complete, the next step is **mounting the key electrical and mechanical components** in an optimal configuration.

Motor Mounting

The motor must be mounted **rigidly to prevent vibrations** and misalignment. **Hub motors** are installed within the rear wheel, requiring minimal mounting effort, whereas **mid-drive motors** require a dedicated mounting bracket.

Motor Type	**Mounting Position**	**Advantages**	**Challenges**
Hub Motor	Inside rear wheel	No chains or belts	Less torque
Mid-Drive Motor	Near bottom bracket	Higher torque, better weight distribution	Requires custom mounting

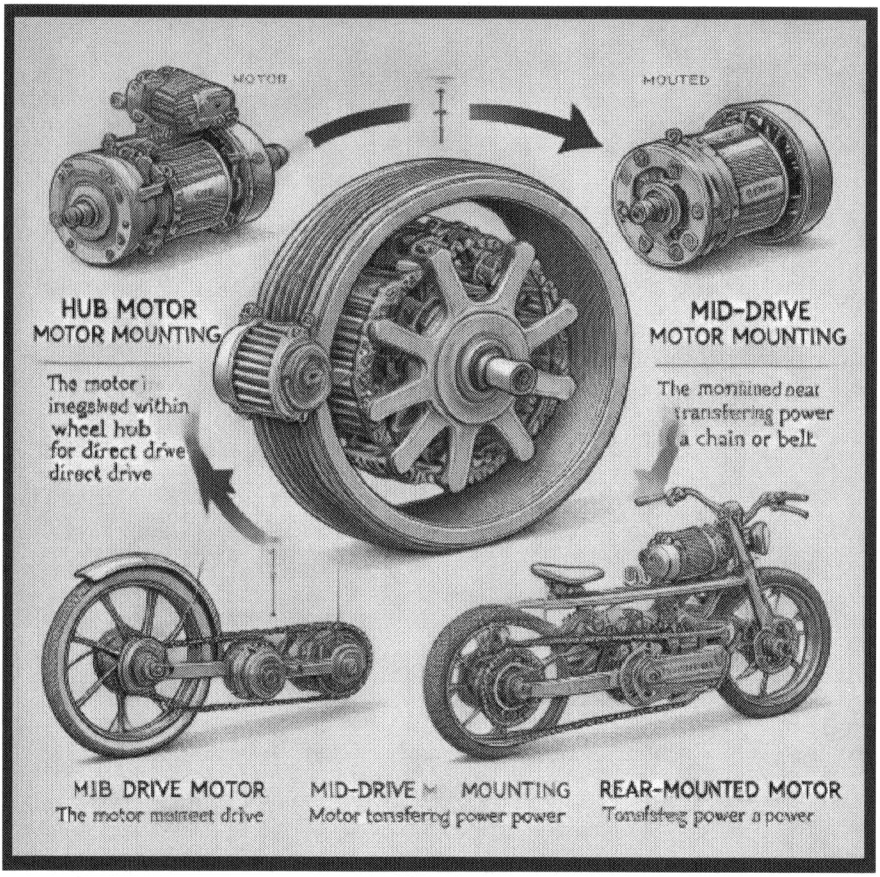

Figure 15 Different motor mounting configurations

Battery Pack Positioning

The battery pack is one of the **heaviest components** and must be placed **low in the frame for stability**. Common battery mounting positions include:

- **Under the seat or within the frame's central triangle** (ideal for bicycles).
- **On the floorboard** (common for electric scooters).
- **Inside a reinforced battery box** for protection against shocks and weather.

The **battery mounting system should include shock absorbers** to reduce vibrations and ensure **proper ventilation to prevent overheating**.

Controller and Wiring Layout

The motor controller should be **placed in a ventilated location** to avoid overheating. Common locations include:

- **Behind the battery pack**
- **Under the seat**
- **Within a custom electronics enclosure**

Proper **cable management** is essential for safety and aesthetics. Wires should be **secured using cable ties and protective tubing** to prevent wear and accidental disconnections.

Building the chassis and frame is one of the most crucial steps in constructing an electric two-wheeler. The choice between **fabricating a custom frame or modifying an existing one** depends on the **builder's skill level, budget, and design preferences**. Careful consideration must be given to **material selection,**

weight distribution, and structural reinforcements. Proper mounting of the **motor, battery, and controller** ensures long-term durability and optimal performance.

With the chassis and frame completed, the next step in the DIY electric two-wheeler project will involve **integrating the powertrain, including motor installation, drivetrain setup, and electrical wiring** to bring the vehicle to life.

Chapter 6

Choosing and Installing the Electric Motor

The **electric motor** is the **heart of an electric two-wheeler**, converting electrical energy from the battery into mechanical energy to propel the vehicle. Choosing the right motor is critical, as it determines the **speed, torque, efficiency, and overall performance** of the bike or scooter. This chapter explores how to **select, mount, and wire** the motor to ensure optimal operation.

Selecting the Right Motor

Choosing an appropriate motor involves **analyzing various factors**, such as the required power output, torque, efficiency, and weight. The two most common types of electric motors used in two-wheelers are **hub motors and mid-drive motors**, each offering unique advantages and trade-offs.

1. Power Ratings

The power of an electric motor is measured in **watts (W)**, which defines how much energy it can convert per second. Power directly influences **acceleration, top speed, and load-carrying capacity**.

Motor Power (W)	**Use Case**	**Estimated Top Speed (km/h)**	**Suitable Terrain**
250W -	Lightweight e-	25-40 km/h	Flat roads

Motor Power (W)	Use Case	Estimated Top Speed (km/h)	Suitable Terrain
500W	bikes, city commuting		
750W - 1000W	Medium-sized e-bikes, scooters	40-55 km/h	Urban and mild inclines
1500W - 3000W	High-performance scooters, motorbikes	55-80 km/h	Hilly terrain, off-road
5000W+	Electric motorcycles	80+ km/h	High-speed roads, racing

The power should be selected based on the **intended usage**. For a **lightweight commuter vehicle**, a **500W or 750W motor** is ideal, while an **off-road or high-speed electric bike** requires **1500W or higher**.

2. Torque and Efficiency

Torque is measured in **Newton-meters (Nm)** and determines how much **force the motor can apply to the wheels**. Higher torque is essential for **hill climbing and carrying heavy loads**.

Motor Type	Torque Output (Nm)	Efficiency (%)	Best For
Hub Motor	40-90 Nm	80-88%	City riding, simplicity
Mid-Drive Motor	60-120 Nm	85-92%	Off-road, climbing hills

Mid-drive motors generally provide **higher torque** than hub motors, making them more efficient for hilly terrains and uneven roads. However, **hub motors are simpler to install and maintain** since they don't require chains or belts.

Mounting the Motor

Once the motor is selected, the next step is installation. The mounting process varies based on whether you are using a **hub motor** or a **mid-drive motor**.

1. Hub Motor Installation

A hub motor is installed directly within the wheel, either in the **front or rear**. Rear hub motors offer better traction and stability, while front hub motors provide **simpler installation** and **better weight distribution**.

Steps to Install a Hub Motor:

Remove the existing wheel from the frame and replace it with the hub motor wheel.

Secure the axle inside the dropouts of the frame. Use **torque arms** to prevent axle spin under load.

Tighten the nuts and washers securely to keep the motor in place.

Route the motor wiring carefully, avoiding sharp bends or potential pinch points.

Pros of Hub Motors	**Cons of Hub Motors**
Easy installation	Higher unsprung weight affects suspension
No need for chains or gears	Difficult to repair a flat tire
Low maintenance	Less torque compared to mid-drive

2. Mid-Drive Motor Installation

Mid-drive motors are installed **at the bike's crank**, transferring power through the **chain or belt drive**. These motors provide **better weight distribution** and **higher torque**, making them ideal for **performance-oriented electric two-wheelers**.

Steps to Install a Mid-Drive Motor:

1. **Remove the existing bottom bracket** and crankset from the frame.
2. **Insert the motor unit** into the bottom bracket shell, ensuring a snug fit.
3. **Secure the motor with mounting bolts** and torque them to specification.
4. **Reinstall the chain and chainring**, ensuring proper alignment.
5. **Connect the motor's wiring** to the controller and throttle system.

Pros of Mid-Drive Motors	Cons of Mid-Drive Motors
High torque and efficiency	More complex installation
Uses existing gears for variable speed	Requires chain or belt maintenance
Better weight distribution	Can wear out drivetrain components

Wiring the Motor

Once the motor is physically installed, the final step is **electrical wiring**. The motor connects to the **controller**, which regulates power from the battery and responds to the throttle and braking system.

1. Identifying Motor Wires

Most motors have the following key wires:

- **Phase Wires (Thick Wires - Blue, Yellow, Green):** These carry high-power signals to drive the motor.
- **Hall Sensor Wires (Thin Wires - Red, Black, Yellow, Green, Blue):** These provide feedback to the controller for precise motor operation.
- **Power Wires (Red & Black):** These connect to the battery.

A **table summarizing wire functions** can help users understand wiring color codes.

Wire Type	**Function**	**Typical Colors**
Phase Wires	Drive the motor	Blue, Yellow, Green
Hall Sensor Wires	Feedback signals	Red, Black, Yellow, Green, Blue
Power Wires	Supply power	Red (+), Black (-)

2. Connecting to the Controller

Connect the phase wires from the motor to the corresponding phase terminals on the controller.

Plug in the hall sensor wires into the controller's hall sensor port.

Attach the battery power wires to the controller's input terminals, ensuring correct polarity.

Connect the throttle and brake sensors to the controller's respective input ports.

3. Testing the Motor

After wiring, it's essential to **test the motor before full operation**.

Power on the system and ensure all connections are secure.

Turn the throttle slowly and observe motor rotation.

Check for error codes on the controller, which might indicate faulty connections.

Ensure smooth acceleration and braking without unusual noises or vibrations.

The electric motor plays a **vital role in determining the performance of an electric two-wheeler**, making it essential to **select the right type, install it properly, and ensure a reliable wiring connection**. While **hub motors offer simplicity and ease of installation**, **mid-drive motors provide better torque and efficiency** for demanding applications.

Chapter 7

Battery Pack Assembly and Management

The **battery pack** is the **energy source** of an electric two-wheeler, storing electrical power and supplying it to the motor through the controller. Selecting the **right battery technology**, determining the **ideal configuration**, and ensuring **safe assembly** are critical for optimizing performance, efficiency, and longevity. This chapter provides a detailed understanding of **battery types, pack design, configuration methods, and management techniques**, allowing builders to construct a reliable and high-performance battery pack for their DIY electric vehicle.

Choosing Battery Cells

The choice of battery technology determines the overall efficiency, weight, cost, and lifespan of an electric two-wheeler. While various battery chemistries are available, **Lithium-ion (Li-ion)** and **Lithium Iron Phosphate (LiFePO4)** are the most commonly used due to their high energy density, efficiency, and relatively long lifespan.

Comparison of Different Battery Types

Battery Type	**Energy Density (Wh/kg)**	**Lifespan (Charge Cycles)**	**Weight**	**Safety**	**Cost**	**Best Used For**
Li-ion (Lithium-ion - NMC, NCA)	150-250	500-1000	Light	Moderate	High	High-performance e-bikes, scooters
LiFePO4 (Lithium Iron Phosphate)	90-140	2000-5000	Heavy	Very Safe	Moderate	Long-life applications, electric motorcycles
Lead-Acid	30-50	300-500	Very Heavy	Low	Low	Budget builds, low-speed e-scooters
NiMH (Nickel-Metal Hydride)	60-120	500-800	Moderate	Moderate	High	Rarely used today due to lower efficiency

For **high-performance electric two-wheelers**, **Li-ion batteries** (such as **NMC - Nickel Manganese Cobalt** and **NCA - Nickel Cobalt Aluminum**) are preferred because of their **lightweight construction and high power output**. However, they **require a Battery Management System (BMS)** to prevent overcharging and overheating.

For **safety-focused and long-lasting designs**, **LiFePO4 batteries** are an excellent choice. They have a **longer lifespan and greater thermal stability**, reducing the risk of fires or thermal runaway. However, they **weigh more** and have **lower energy density** than Li-ion cells.

Battery Pack Configuration

Building a battery pack involves arranging individual cells into a **series, parallel, or a combination of both** to achieve the desired **voltage (V)** and **capacity (Ah)**.

Understanding Battery Cell Ratings

Each individual battery cell has a specific **voltage and capacity** rating. For example:

- **Li-ion 18650 cells (most common)**:
  - **Nominal Voltage = 3.6V**
  - **Capacity = 2500mAh to 3500mAh**

- **LiFePO4 cells (e.g., 32700 format):**
    - **Nominal Voltage = 3.2V**
    - **Capacity = 6000mAh to 10000mAh**

A **battery pack must be designed** to provide the **required voltage and capacity** for an electric two-wheeler.

Series Configuration – Increasing Voltage

Connecting **cells in series (S)** increases the total **voltage** while maintaining the **same capacity**.

Formula:

Vtotal=Vcell×Number of Cells in SeriesV_{\ {total}} = V_{\ {cell}} \times \ {Number of Cells in Series}Vtotal=Vcell ×Number of Cells in Series Ahtotal=Ahindividual cellAh_{\ {total}} = Ah_{\ {individual cell}}Ahtotal=Ahindividual cell

For example, if we connect **13 Li-ion cells (3.6V each) in series**, we get:

3.6V×13=46.8V3.6V \times 13 = 46.8V3.6V×13=46.8V

This is commonly referred to as a **"13S" configuration**, typically used for **48V e-bike battery packs**.

Parallel Configuration – Increasing Capacity

Connecting **cells in parallel (P)** increases the total **capacity (Ah)** while maintaining the **same voltage**.

Formula:

Ahtotal=Ahcell×Number of Parallel CellsAh_{\ {total}} = Ah_{\ {cell}} \times \ {Number of Parallel Cells}Ahtotal =Ahcell×Number of Parallel Cells Vtotal=VcellV_{\ {total}} = V_{\ {cell}}Vtotal=Vcell

For example, if each **cell has 3Ah** capacity and we connect **4 cells in parallel**, the total capacity becomes:

3Ah×4=12Ah3Ah \times 4 = 12Ah3Ah×4=12Ah

This is referred to as a "**4P**" **configuration**, meaning **4 cells are connected in parallel** to increase battery runtime.

Combining Series and Parallel

A complete battery pack is designed using a combination of **series and parallel** connections.

For a **48V, 20Ah battery pack**, a **13S4P configuration** would be used:

- **13 cells in series** to achieve **48V**

- **4 parallel groups** to achieve **20Ah total capacity**

Example Configuration Table for a 48V 20Ah Pack (Li-ion 18650 cells, 3.6V, 3Ah per cell):

Number of Series Cells (S)	Number of Parallel Cells (P)	Total Voltage (V)	Total Capacity (Ah)
13	1	48V	3Ah
13	2	48V	6Ah
13	4	48V	12Ah
13	6	48V	18Ah
13	7	48V	21Ah

Key Considerations for Battery Pack

Proper **battery pack design and management** ensure **safety, longevity, and efficiency**. Here are the critical aspects to consider:

1. **Battery Cell Matching**
   - Use **identical cells** with the **same voltage, capacity, and internal resistance** to prevent imbalances.
2. **Spot Welding vs. Soldering**

- **Spot welding** is preferred as it provides strong connections without overheating the cells. **Soldering can damage the battery cells** due to excessive heat.

3. **Battery Management System (BMS)**
   - A **BMS is required** to **balance the cells**, **prevent overcharging**, **over-discharging**, and **monitor temperature**.
4. **Thermal Management**
   - Use **heat sinks or active cooling** for high-power battery packs to prevent overheating. **Li-ion cells generate heat during discharge** and need proper ventilation.
5. **Battery Enclosure & Safety**
   - **Fire-resistant and lightweight materials** should be used for the **battery casing** to protect against mechanical damage and thermal runaway.

The **battery pack** is one of the most crucial and expensive components of an electric two-wheeler. Understanding **different battery chemistries, designing the right series-parallel configuration, and implementing a proper BMS system** ensures maximum **efficiency, longevity, and safety**.

A well-designed battery pack will provide **long range, high performance, and reliable power delivery**, making the electric two-wheeler **efficient and practical** for daily commuting or high-speed applications.

Battery Management System (BMS)

An electric two-wheeler relies on an efficient **Battery Management System (BMS)** and a **proper charging system** to ensure longevity, safety, and optimal performance of the battery pack. The BMS plays a crucial role in **cell balancing, monitoring, and protecting the battery pack**, while the charging system ensures the battery is recharged efficiently without overheating or overcharging. This chapter will explore the **importance of a BMS, how it is wired, troubleshooting common issues, selecting the right charger, and best practices for safe charging**.

Battery Management System (BMS)

The **Battery Management System (BMS)** is an essential component of any lithium-based battery pack. It prevents common battery failures such as **overcharging, over-discharging, short circuits, overheating, and cell imbalance**. Without a BMS, the battery pack can suffer from **reduced lifespan, efficiency loss, or catastrophic failures like thermal runaway**.

Functions of a BMS

A BMS performs several critical functions:

Voltage Regulation: It ensures that each cell in the battery pack operates within its safe voltage range. Overcharging or over-discharging a single cell can cause permanent damage.

Cell Balancing: Lithium cells can have slight variations in capacity, leading to imbalances over time. The BMS **redistributes charge** across cells to ensure they all remain at equal voltage levels.

Temperature Monitoring: Excessive heat can degrade battery performance and safety. The BMS **monitors temperature sensors** and can disconnect the pack if overheating is detected.

Current Protection: It prevents excessive **discharge current**, which can damage cells and the electrical system of the two-wheeler.

Short-Circuit Protection: If a **short circuit** occurs, the BMS instantly cuts off power to prevent fire hazards or damage.

State of Charge (SOC) Estimation: The BMS estimates how much charge remains in the battery pack, ensuring an accurate battery level display.

Types of BMS Systems

There are two primary types of BMS used in electric two-wheelers:

Type	Description	Pros	Cons
Passive BMS	Uses resistors to burn off excess energy from higher-voltage cells to balance them.	Simple, cost-effective, widely used.	Wastes energy as heat, slower balancing.
Active BMS	Redistributes excess charge from higher-voltage cells to lower-voltage ones.	More efficient, extends battery life, minimizes energy loss.	More expensive, complex circuitry.

For **DIY electric two-wheelers**, a **passive BMS** is usually sufficient if **high efficiency is not required**. However, for high-performance applications, an **active BMS** can be beneficial.

Wiring the BMS to the Battery Pack

A **BMS is connected** to the battery pack through **balance leads and power connections**. The **balance leads** are responsible for monitoring each individual cell's voltage, while the **main power wires** control the charge and discharge processes.

Typical BMS Wiring Steps for a 13S Li-ion Battery Pack (48V)

1. **Identify the BMS Terminals**
   - **B- (Battery Negative)**: Connects to the main negative terminal of the battery pack.
   - **P- (Power Negative)**: Connects to the controller's negative input.
   - **C- (Charge Negative)**: Connects to the charger's negative terminal.
   - **B1, B2, B3... (Balance Leads)**: Connected to individual battery groups to monitor voltage.
2. **Connect the Balance Leads**
   - Each balance lead wire is connected to the **positive terminal** of each series group in the battery pack.
   - The first wire (B1) connects to **the first series connection**, the second wire (B2) to the next, and so on.
3. **Connect the Main Power Wires**
   - The **B- terminal** of the BMS is soldered to the **battery pack's main negative terminal**.
   - The **P- terminal** is connected to the load (controller or motor).
   - The **C- terminal** is connected to the charger's negative output.
4. **Secure and Insulate the Wiring**
   - Ensure all connections are **properly insulated** with **heat shrink tubing** or electrical tape to prevent short circuits.
5. **Test the System**

- Use a **multimeter** to verify that each balance lead is properly connected and that the **pack voltage matches the expected total**.

Common BMS Issues and Troubleshooting

A **malfunctioning BMS** can cause various problems, including **battery not charging, unbalanced cells, or system shut-offs**. Below is a table detailing common issues and solutions:

Problem	**Possible Cause**	**Solution**
Battery pack not charging	BMS cutoff due to overvoltage	Check each cell voltage; ensure charger is within range
Battery drains too fast	Cell imbalance, defective BMS	Replace defective cells or recalibrate BMS
Electric two-wheeler suddenly turns off	Overcurrent protection triggered	Reduce load, check connections for short circuits
Battery not providing full power	Weak cell group in series	Identify weak cells and replace

Charging System

A **proper charging system** is necessary to keep the battery pack in **good health** while preventing **overheating, overcharging, and damage**. Selecting the right charger ensures the battery charges **efficiently and safely**.

Choosing the Right Charger

A charger must match the **voltage and chemistry** of the battery pack. The most critical parameters to consider are:

Battery Voltage (Pack Configuration)	**Recommended Charger Voltage**	**Charging Current**
36V (10S Li-ion)	42V	2A – 5A
48V (13S Li-ion)	54.6V	2A – 5A
60V (16S Li-ion)	67.2V	3A – 8A
72V (20S Li-ion)	84V	5A – 10A

A **higher charging current** speeds up charging but generates **more heat**, which can reduce battery lifespan. It is recommended to **charge at 0.5C to 1C rate** (where C is the battery capacity).

Safe Charging Practices

1. **Use the Manufacturer-Recommended Charger**
   - Always use a charger that matches the **battery's voltage and chemistry**.
   - A **Li-ion charger** should not be used for **LiFePO4** batteries and vice versa.
2. **Charge in a Well-Ventilated Area**
   - Charging generates heat, so **avoid charging in enclosed spaces** or near flammable materials.
3. **Avoid Overcharging**
   - Never leave the battery **plugged in for extended periods**.
   - A **BMS with overcharge protection** will automatically cut off charging when the battery is full.
4. **Monitor Temperature**
   - If the **battery becomes excessively hot** during charging, stop charging immediately and inspect for faults.
5. **Periodic Full Charge and Balancing**
   - Occasionally **charge the battery to 100%** to allow the **BMS to balance the cells properly**.

The **Battery Management System (BMS) and charging system** are essential for the safety and longevity of an electric two-wheeler's battery pack. A **properly wired BMS** ensures **cell balancing,**

overcurrent protection, and thermal monitoring, while a **well-chosen charger** prevents overcharging and maximizes battery life. By **following correct wiring, troubleshooting common issues, and adopting safe charging habits**, DIY builders can ensure their electric two-wheeler operates reliably and efficiently.

Chapter 8

Motor Controller & Throttle System

An electric two-wheeler's performance is largely dictated by its **motor controller and throttle system**. The motor controller acts as the **brain of the propulsion system**, regulating the flow of electrical power from the battery to the motor. It dictates how the motor responds to **acceleration, braking, and varying load conditions**, ensuring **smooth and efficient** operation.

The **throttle system** serves as the **interface between the rider and the vehicle's power system**, determining how the motor responds to user input. A well-calibrated throttle system ensures **seamless acceleration and deceleration**, preventing jerky movements and improving ride comfort.

This chapter will cover **motor controller types, programming techniques, installation guidelines, and the proper way to wire and calibrate the throttle system**.

Understanding Motor Controllers

A **motor controller** is an **electronic device** that **regulates the speed, torque, and efficiency** of the motor. It determines how much power is delivered based on input from the **throttle, sensors, and battery management system**.

The main function of a motor controller is to **convert DC power from the battery into an AC or pulsed DC form**, depending on the motor type. It also manages **regenerative braking**, which converts excess kinetic energy back into stored electrical energy.

Types of Motor Controllers

Electric two-wheelers use two primary types of motor controllers:

Controller Type	**Description**	**Pros**	**Cons**
Square Wave Controllers	Uses simple on/off switching (PWM) to regulate motor speed.	Low cost, easy to install, widely available.	Noisy operation, lower efficiency, rough acceleration.
Sine Wave Controllers	Generates a smooth sinusoidal signal for motor operation.	Silent operation, high efficiency, smoother acceleration.	More expensive, requires fine-tuning, complex circuitry.

A **sine wave controller** is **recommended** for DIY electric two-wheelers, as it ensures **silent operation,**

better efficiency, and improved ride comfort. However, **square wave controllers** are still useful in budget applications where cost is a major concern.

Programming the Motor Controller

Most **modern motor controllers** allow for software-based tuning, which helps **optimize performance** based on the user's needs. The **key parameters** that can be adjusted include:

1. **Throttle Sensitivity**: Determines how fast the motor responds to acceleration inputs.
2. **Maximum Current Limit**: Prevents excessive current draw from the battery, protecting it from overheating.
3. **Regenerative Braking Strength**: Adjusts how much energy is recovered during braking.
4. **Acceleration Curve**: Defines whether acceleration should be linear or gradual for better rider control.
5. **Speed Limits**: Some controllers allow setting different speed limits for safety or regulatory compliance.

Most controllers have **PC or smartphone-based tuning interfaces**, allowing users to fine-tune these settings via **USB, Bluetooth, or serial connections**. Proper tuning ensures **better energy efficiency, longer battery life, and smoother acceleration**.

Installing the Controller

The placement of the **motor controller** is critical for **heat dissipation, protection, and ease of wiring**. It must be **securely mounted** to prevent vibrations from loosening connections.

Choosing the Right Mounting Location

1. **Away from Heat Sources**: The controller generates heat and must be mounted in a **well-ventilated area**.
2. **Easily Accessible for Maintenance**: If firmware updates or wiring modifications are needed, the controller should be in a location that is easy to access.
3. **Protected from Water and Dust**: If riding in **wet or dusty conditions**, ensure the controller is inside a **sealed or weatherproof housing**.

Mounting Steps

1. **Select the Mounting Surface**: The best options are **inside the chassis frame or beneath the seat**.
2. **Drill Mounting Holes**: Use **pre-drilled mounting brackets** or **custom-fabricated plates** to securely hold the controller.
3. **Attach Using Bolts or Clamps**: Ensure the unit is tightly secured but with enough clearance for airflow.

4. **Use Thermal Pads or Heatsinks**: If the controller tends to overheat, **install a heatsink or cooling fan** to improve heat dissipation.

Connecting the Throttle

The **throttle system** is the primary interface that controls **power delivery to the motor**. It is connected directly to the **motor controller**, sending voltage signals that regulate acceleration.

Types of Throttle Systems

Throttle Type	**Description**	**Pros**	**Cons**
Hall Effect Throttle	Uses magnetic sensors to detect movement.	Smooth, precise control, durable.	Requires proper calibration, sensitive to damage.
Resistive Throttle (Potentiometer-Based)	Uses a variable resistor to adjust voltage.	Simple, low-cost, widely available.	Less accurate, susceptible to wear over time.

A **Hall effect throttle** is **preferred** for modern electric two-wheelers due to **its accuracy, durability, and smooth control**.

Wiring the Throttle to the Controller

The throttle generally has **three wires**, which must be connected to the controller:

Wire Color	**Function**	**Connection**
Red	5V Power Supply	Connects to the 5V output of the motor controller.
Black	Ground	Connects to the GND terminal of the controller.
Green (or White)	Signal Wire	Connects to the throttle input terminal of the controller.

Calibration and Testing

Once the throttle is wired, calibration is necessary to ensure **smooth acceleration and no dead zones**. The process involves:

Powering on the System: Turn on the battery and controller.

Checking Idle Voltage: Use a **multimeter** to ensure the **throttle signal starts at 0.8V – 1.0V** at rest.

Testing Full Acceleration: Fully twist the throttle and check that the signal **does not exceed 4.2V – 4.5V**.

Adjusting the Response Curve: If the acceleration is too aggressive, adjust it through **controller programming settings**.

Ensuring Smooth Power Delivery: Gradually twist the throttle and observe the **motor response** to confirm there are no sudden jerks or delays.

Safety Considerations

Ensuring **safe operation** of the motor controller and throttle system is crucial for **preventing electrical failures, unwanted acceleration, and overheating**.

Preventing Throttle Malfunctions

1. **Use Waterproof Connectors**: Moisture can cause short circuits or erratic acceleration.
2. **Check for Loose Wiring**: Vibrations from riding can loosen connections over time, leading to throttle failures.

3. **Install a Kill Switch**: A dedicated emergency kill switch ensures that the motor can be instantly turned off in case of a malfunction.

Ensuring Motor Controller Longevity

1. **Avoid Overloading**: Do not exceed the controller's **rated power output**, as excessive current draw can cause overheating.
2. **Regularly Update Firmware**: If the controller supports software updates, ensure it has the latest firmware for optimized performance.
3. **Monitor Heat Levels**: If the controller becomes excessively hot, add **a cooling fan or reposition it for better airflow**.

The **motor controller and throttle system** are the heart of an electric two-wheeler's performance. A **properly selected and installed controller** ensures efficient power delivery, while a **well-calibrated throttle system** provides a smooth and responsive riding experience.

By understanding **controller programming, optimal wiring techniques, and safety considerations**, DIY builders can ensure their electric two-wheeler operates **reliably, safely, and efficiently**.

Chapter 9

Wiring & Electronics Integration

A **well-designed wiring system** is the backbone of any **electric two-wheeler**, ensuring that **power flows efficiently and safely** between all components. Proper **electronics integration** not only enhances performance but also **prevents electrical failures**, **improves battery efficiency**, and **ensures rider safety**.

This chapter will provide a **comprehensive wiring guide**, covering **essential circuit diagrams, fuse protection mechanisms, wire gauge selection, and cable management techniques**. Understanding the **electrical interconnections** is crucial for ensuring **optimal functionality, reliability, and safety**.

Essential Wiring Diagram

An **electric two-wheeler** consists of **multiple electronic components** that must be **properly wired** to function correctly. Below is a **basic schematic** that outlines the **connections between the battery, motor controller, throttle, display, brake system, and other essential elements**.

Overview of Key Electrical Components

Every electric two-wheeler requires a **structured wiring layout** to ensure **smooth communication between different components**. Below is a **table** that highlights the key electrical components and their function:

Component	Function
Battery Pack	Stores electrical energy and supplies power to all components.
Motor Controller	Regulates power flow from the battery to the motor based on user input.
Electric Motor	Converts electrical energy into mechanical motion to propel the vehicle.
Throttle System	Sends acceleration signals to the controller.
Brake Cut-Off Switch	Disables motor power when brakes are engaged.
Fuse & Circuit Breaker	Protects wiring from overcurrent conditions.
DC-DC Converter	Converts high battery voltage to lower voltage for accessories like lights, displays, and USB chargers.

Component	Function
Display Panel	Shows battery status, speed, and power usage.

Basic Wiring

The following wiring diagram provides a **visual representation of how all major electrical components interconnect**. The **battery pack**, **motor controller**, and **throttle system** form the **primary power circuit**, while **secondary circuits handle lighting, accessories, and safety features**.

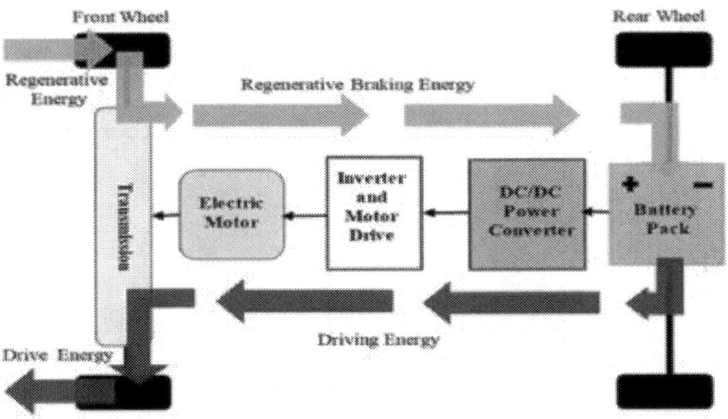

Figure 16 Wiring Diagra

Choosing the Right Wire Gauge and Connectors

The **selection of wire gauge** (thickness) plays a **crucial role in preventing voltage drops and**

overheating. If the wires are too **thin**, they may **overheat**, leading to **short circuits and power loss**. Conversely, **oversized wires** increase **costs and weight unnecessarily**.

Recommended Wire Gauge Selection

Component	**Current Draw (A)**	**Recommended Wire Gauge (AWG)**
Battery to Controller	30-80A	8 - 12 AWG
Controller to Motor	30-100A	8 - 10 AWG
Throttle Wiring	<5A	20 - 22 AWG
Brake Switches	<5A	18 - 22 AWG
Lighting and Accessories	1-10A	16 - 20 AWG

The **length of wiring** also affects the **current carrying capacity**. For longer distances, a **lower gauge (thicker) wire** is necessary to minimize **voltage drop**.

Fuse & Protection Systems

An **electric two-wheeler's wiring system** must be **protected against excessive currents, voltage**

surges, and accidental short circuits. This is achieved using **fuses, circuit breakers, and surge protection devices**.

Why Protection is Necessary?

1. **Prevents Short Circuits**: A short circuit can **damage components** and **cause fires**. Fuses act as a **first line of defense**.
2. **Limits Overcurrent Damage**: If too much current flows due to a **faulty motor or controller**, a **circuit breaker or fuse cuts off power**, protecting the system.
3. **Enhances Battery Life**: Proper protection prevents **battery over-discharge**, which can lead to **permanent damage**.

Fuse Selection for Different Components

Circuit Type	**Recommended Fuse Type**	**Fuse Rating (A)**
Battery Main Line	ANL or Mega Fuse	80 - 150A
Motor Controller	Blade or ANL Fuse	50 - 100A
Lighting System	Mini Blade Fuse	10 - 15A
Charging Circuit	Inline Fuse	10 - 30A

The **main fuse** should be installed **as close to the battery as possible** to provide **maximum protection**.

Safe Wiring Practices

A well-organized **wiring harness** is critical for ensuring **durability and ease of maintenance**. Poor wiring practices can lead to **performance issues, short circuits, or even complete system failures**.

Guidelines for Wiring

1. **Use High-Quality Connectors**: Secure **Anderson Powerpole, XT60, or XT90 connectors** prevent **loose connections and overheating**.
2. **Keep Wiring Short and Direct**: **Minimize unnecessary wire length** to **reduce resistance and voltage drops**.
3. **Label All Wires**: Use **heat-shrink labels** or color coding for **easy troubleshooting**.
4. **Bundle Wires Properly**: Use **corrugated tubing** or **cable sleeves** to keep wires organized and protected.
5. **Avoid Sharp Bends**: Sharp bends in wiring can **cause internal fractures**, leading to **power losses**.
6. **Separate High-Current and Low-Current Wires**: Running **motor wires too close to signal wires** can cause **electromagnetic interference (EMI)**.

Testing the Electrical System Before First Use

Before **powering on the system**, a **thorough inspection and testing phase** is essential to avoid potential damage or safety hazards.

Checklist for Pre-Startup Testing

Test Type	**Procedure**	**Expected Result**
Continuity Check	Use a multimeter to check that wires are properly connected.	No open circuits.
Voltage Check	Measure battery voltage at different points in the circuit.	Consistent readings matching system specifications.
Throttle Response	Slowly twist the throttle and monitor motor response.	Smooth acceleration without delays.
Brake Cut-Off Test	Apply brakes and check if the motor cuts off.	Motor should stop instantly.
Fuse Testing	Remove and inspect fuses for continuity.	Fuses should be intact unless a fault occurred.

A **properly designed wiring and electronics integration system** is essential for ensuring that an **electric two-wheeler operates safely, efficiently, and reliably**. By **following best practices in wiring, selecting the right fuses, and conducting thorough pre-startup testing**, DIY builders can create an **optimized and long-lasting electrical system**.

Chapter 10

Lighting & Instrumentation for an Electric Two Wheeler

A well-designed **lighting and instrumentation system** is crucial for an electric two-wheeler, ensuring **safety, visibility, and real-time monitoring** of critical vehicle parameters. Properly installed **headlights, brake lights, turn signals, and dashboard displays** enhance both **rider safety and user experience**, making the vehicle more practical for daily use.

This chapter explores the **technical aspects of lighting, wiring configurations, power management, and sensor integration**, helping builders design a **functional, efficient, and durable** system.

Lighting & Indicators

Lighting plays a **dual role** in an electric two-wheeler: it **illuminates the road for the rider** and **makes the vehicle visible to others**, especially in **low-light conditions**. The **selection, positioning, and wiring** of lighting components should be done carefully to ensure **optimal visibility without excessive power consumption**.

Types of Lights

Light Type	Purpose	Common Power Ratings	Placement
Headlights	Illuminate the road ahead	10W - 50W (LED preferred)	Front, mounted on the handlebar or chassis
Brake Lights	Alert vehicles behind when braking	5W - 15W (LED)	Rear, above or near the wheel

Light Type	Purpose	Common Power Ratings	Placement
Turn Signals	Indicate turning direction	3W - 10W (Amber LED)	Front and rear sides
Tail Lights	Improve rear visibility at night	5W - 10W (Red LED)	Rear fender or near battery compartment
Daytime Running Lights (DRLs)	Increase visibility during daylight	3W - 8W (White LED)	Integrated with headlight or separate strip

Choosing the Right Headlight

Headlights are among the most **power-intensive components** of an electric two-wheeler. The ideal **headlight selection** depends on factors such as **brightness (measured in lumens), power efficiency, beam angle, and durability**.

Comparison of Common Headlight Types

Headlight Type	Brightness (Lumens)	Power Consumption	Lifespan	Recommended Use
Halogen Bulbs	400 - 1000 lm	25W - 50W	500 - 1000 hrs	Not recommended due to high power consumption
HID (Xenon)	3000 - 5000 lm	35W - 50W	2000 - 5000 hrs	High-end vehicles, expensive and complex
LED (Recommended)	1500 - 5000 lm	10W - 30W	20,000 + hrs	Most efficient, best for electric vehicles

Among these, **LED headlights** are the **best option** for an electric two-wheeler due to their **low power consumption, high brightness, and long lifespan**. They also produce **less heat**, making them safer to use.

Wiring and Installing Lights

For an efficient and safe **lighting system**, a well-structured **wiring layout** is necessary. The lighting circuit should be designed **to minimize voltage drop, prevent flickering, and integrate with the vehicle's power system efficiently**.

A **basic lighting circuit** consists of:

1. **Power Source** – Direct connection to the **battery** through a **fuse**.
2. **Switches & Relays** – Control the **on/off operation** of lights and indicators.
3. **LED Driver or Regulator** – Ensures stable voltage for LEDs.
4. **Wiring & Connectors** – Properly insulated wires prevent **short circuits and voltage drops**.

Brake Light and Turn Signal Integration

Brake lights must activate **instantly** when the brake lever is engaged, warning vehicles behind. The brake system can be connected via:

- **Mechanical Switch**: A small switch near the brake lever that **closes the circuit when the brake is applied**.
- **Electronic Sensor**: A pressure-sensitive switch that **detects brake application electronically**.

For **turn signals**, a **flasher relay or microcontroller-based module** ensures the **blinking function**. These indicators should be **highly visible** and **placed at the right height** to be noticeable in traffic.

Display & Instrumentation

A **dashboard display** serves as the **central control panel** for the electric two-wheeler, providing the rider with **real-time information on speed, battery level, motor status, and additional diagnostics**.

Key Display Components

Instrument	**Function**	**Display Type**
Speedometer	Displays vehicle speed	Digital LCD or Analog
Battery Meter	Shows remaining charge and voltage level	LED bar, LCD percentage display
Odometer	Tracks total distance traveled	Digital LCD
Trip Meter	Tracks distance per ride session	Digital LCD
Motor	Alerts overheating	Digital

Instrument	Function	Display Type
Temperature Sensor	issues	thermometer
Controller Error Code Display	Shows fault codes for troubleshooting	LCD with error messages

Selecting the Right Display

The **choice of display** depends on factors such as **power efficiency, readability, and durability**. Modern **LCD and OLED displays** are widely used due to their **low power consumption and clear readability in daylight**.

Comparison of Common Display Types

Display Type	Power Consumption	Readability	Durability	Use Case
Analog Gauge	Low	Moderate	High	Simple, low-cost setups
Monochrome LCD	Very Low	Good	Moderate	Basic speed and battery

Display Type	Power Consumption	Readability	Durability	Use Case
				meters
Color TFT LCD	Moderate	Excellent	Moderate	Advanced dashboards
OLED Display	Low	Excellent	High	Premium electric vehicles

Integrating Sensors for Better Monitoring

Modern electric two-wheelers can be equipped with **additional sensors** that provide valuable real-time feedback.

Sensor Type	Function	Installation Point
Hall Effect Sensor	Measures wheel rotation to calculate speed	Near wheel hub
Temperature Sensor	Monitors motor/controller temperature	Attached to motor/controller

Sensor Type	Function	Installation Point
Voltage & Current Sensor	Measures battery health and power consumption	Near battery pack
Gyroscope & Accelerometer	Detects vehicle tilt and sudden movements	Frame or dashboard

Wiring and Mounting the Display

A **display module** should be mounted in a position where the **rider can easily view information** without being distracted. The wiring should be connected to:

- **Battery Power Supply** (via a regulated **DC-DC converter**).
- **Controller CAN Bus or UART Port** for data exchange.
- **Hall Sensor & Speed Sensor** to display accurate speed readings.

A **well-designed lighting and instrumentation system** enhances **safety, usability, and rider convenience** in an electric two-wheeler. Properly installed **headlights, brake lights, turn signals, and dashboard displays** ensure that the rider has **full**

control and visibility of their vehicle's status at all times.

Testing & Troubleshooting

After assembling all components of an electric two-wheeler, a thorough **testing and troubleshooting phase** is essential to ensure that the vehicle functions safely and efficiently. Testing not only helps in identifying possible faults but also fine-tunes the performance for better efficiency, acceleration, and battery life. This chapter provides a detailed step-by-step approach for **initial power-up, diagnosing common issues, and optimizing the motor controller for peak performance**.

First Power-Up & Initial Checks

Powering up an electric vehicle for the first time requires a **structured approach** to prevent accidental short circuits, component failures, or hazardous malfunctions. The **initial testing** should be conducted in a **controlled environment**, ideally on a **stand** where the wheels can rotate freely without contact with the ground.

Step-by-Step Guide for First Power-Up

Battery Inspection and Voltage Verification Before connecting the battery to the system, it is crucial to check the output voltage using a **multimeter**. The voltage should match the expected nominal value based on the battery configuration. For instance, a **48V system should read approximately 50-54V when fully charged**. Any deviation may indicate improper wiring or faulty battery cells.

Ensuring Proper Connections and Insulation Each connection should be double-checked to ensure that **polarity is correct**, wires are firmly secured, and insulation is intact. Poor connections or reversed polarity can lead to **component damage, overheating, or even electrical fires**.

Fuse and Safety Check

The vehicle should be equipped with **fuses and circuit breakers** rated for the current draw of the system. A quick continuity test on fuses ensures that they are intact before power-up. If a fuse blows immediately upon turning on the system, there is likely a short circuit that needs immediate attention.

Controller and Motor Test

With the vehicle on a **stand**, the **throttle should be gently engaged** to test whether the motor spins freely. Any **strange noises, excessive vibrations, or lack of movement** could indicate loose wiring, incorrect settings, or motor/controller faults.

Brake and Safety Feature Testing

The **brake cutoff switch** should be tested to ensure that engaging the brakes cuts off power to the motor. If regenerative braking is enabled, the system should be checked for proper energy recovery when braking.

Low-Speed Movement Test

If the initial tests pass, the vehicle can be taken for a **low-speed trial in an open area**. Gradual acceleration, braking, and turning should be tested at **low speeds** to check for **unexpected behavior or lag in throttle response**.

Common Issues & Fixes

Despite careful assembly, various **technical issues** may arise when testing the electric two-wheeler. This section addresses some of the most frequent problems encountered during the first power-up and their solutions.

Diagnosing Motor Issues

Issue	Possible Cause	Solution
Motor does not spin	Loose wiring, controller failure, or blown fuse	Check all connections, replace fuse if necessary, inspect

Issue	Possible Cause	Solution
		controller status LED
Motor vibrates but does not rotate	Incorrect phase wiring, hall sensor malfunction	Swap phase wires, check sensor readings
Overheating motor	Excessive load, poor ventilation	Reduce weight load, ensure airflow to the motor
Motor runs but has low power	Low battery voltage, incorrect controller settings	Charge battery, adjust controller parameters

Troubleshooting Controller Errors

Many **motor controllers** come with built-in **error detection systems**, often indicated by **LED blinks or error codes on the display**.

Error Code	Issue	Solution
E01 - Throttle Fault	Throttle sensor failure	Check wiring, replace throttle if faulty
E02 - Overcurrent	Excessive current draw due to short	Inspect wiring, reduce load, reset

Error Code	Issue	Solution
Protection	circuit or motor issue	controller
E03 - Overvoltage Error	Battery voltage exceeding controller limit	Verify battery voltage, check BMS function
E04 - Undervoltage Error	Battery drained below safe threshold	Recharge battery, check battery health

Battery Faults and Fixes

Symptom	Possible Cause	Solution
Battery not charging	Faulty charger, damaged BMS	Try a different charger, inspect BMS connections
Rapid battery drain	Cell imbalance, excessive load	Perform battery balancing, reduce power consumption
Battery overheating	Overcharging, poor ventilation	Use a fan for cooling, check charging voltage

Performance Optimization

Once the basic system is functional, **fine-tuning the motor controller** can significantly improve **efficiency, range, and riding experience**. Most modern controllers allow adjustments through **PC software, mobile apps, or onboard LCD interfaces**.

Optimizing Acceleration and Torque

A higher **current limit setting** will result in faster acceleration but can reduce battery life. Reducing this setting slightly **improves range** without significantly affecting performance. The **torque sensor sensitivity** should be adjusted for smoother acceleration transitions.

Regenerative Braking Efficiency

Regenerative braking can **recover energy while braking**, extending battery range. However, **excessive regenerative braking force** can cause instability. A moderate setting ensures **smooth deceleration while effectively recharging the battery**.

Voltage and Power Mapping

Many controllers allow **power mapping**, where throttle response is adjusted based on **speed and voltage levels**. Fine-tuning this ensures **linear acceleration** and prevents sudden power surges, improving rider comfort.

Parameter	**Effect on Performance**	**Suggested Setting**
Throttle Sensitivity	High = Instant response, Low = Smooth ride	Medium to High
Regenerative Braking Strength	High = More energy recovery, Low = Smooth deceleration	Medium
Current Limit	High = More torque, Low = More efficiency	Adjust based on battery capacity
Cutoff Voltage	High = Better battery lifespan, Low = More power usage	Recommended per battery specs

Testing and troubleshooting an electric two-wheeler is a **critical phase** that ensures **safety, reliability, and efficiency**. By following **structured power-up procedures**, identifying **common motor, controller, and battery issues**, and **fine-tuning the motor controller**, builders can achieve a **smooth and reliable ride experience**. A properly tested vehicle not only performs efficiently but also **ensures long-term durability and rider safety**.

Chapter 11

Enhancements & Customizations

Once an electric two-wheeler is fully assembled and tested, it becomes possible to enhance its performance by upgrading key components. Performance improvements can include increasing **range, top speed, acceleration, and energy efficiency**. Customizations may involve integrating **advanced braking systems, improved suspension, smart monitoring features, and aesthetic modifications**. This chapter explores **various upgrade paths**, with a special focus on **increasing range and speed** by upgrading battery packs, motor controllers, and motors, as well as implementing **regenerative braking for energy recovery**.

Increasing Range & Speed

The **range** of an electric two-wheeler depends primarily on **battery capacity, motor efficiency, aerodynamics, and weight**. Speed, on the other hand, is influenced by **motor power, controller settings, and wheel configuration**. By upgrading specific components, riders can significantly enhance their vehicle's performance while maintaining safety and efficiency.

Upgrading the Battery Pack

One of the most effective ways to increase range is by upgrading the **battery pack** to a **higher capacity or more energy-dense chemistry**. The table below highlights how different battery types impact range and efficiency.

Battery Type	**Energy Density (Wh/kg)**	**Cycle Life**	**Weight**	**Pros**	**Cons**
Lead-Acid	30-50	300-500 cycles	High	Low cost, readily available	Heavy, short lifespan, low efficiency
Lithium-Ion (Li-ion)	150-250	800-2000 cycles	Medium	Lightweight, high energy density	Expensive, requires BMS
Lithium Iron Phosphate (LiFePO4)	90-160	2000-5000 cycles	Medium	Long lifespan, thermal stability	Slightly lower energy density

Battery Type	Energy Density (Wh/kg)	Cycle Life	Weight	Pros	Cons
Solid-State Battery	300+	1000-3000 cycles	Low	High energy storage, lightweight	Expensive, emerging technology

A typical **48V 20Ah lithium-ion battery pack** can provide a **range of approximately 40-50 km** under normal riding conditions. Upgrading to a **48V 40Ah pack** could effectively **double the range**. Increasing the **voltage** from **48V to 72V** can also boost speed, but requires a **compatible controller and motor** to handle the increased power.

Increasing Speed with Motor and Controller

Speed can be enhanced by either **increasing voltage** or **using a higher-rated motor and controller**. A 1000W motor typically supports speeds up to **40-50 km/h**, while a **2000W or 3000W motor** can push speeds beyond **70 km/h**, provided the battery and controller can handle the power demand. The following table outlines typical motor and controller specifications for different speed ranges.

Motor Power (W)	Voltage (V)	Top Speed (km/h)	Controller Current (A)	Recommended Battery (Ah)
500W	36V	30-40 km/h	20A	20Ah
1000W	48V	40-50 km/h	25A	30Ah
2000W	60V	60-70 km/h	35A	40Ah
3000W	72V	75-90 km/h	45A	50Ah

It is important to **match the controller to the motor power rating**. Using an **underpowered controller** can **limit acceleration and speed**, while an **overpowered controller** can **overheat and damage the motor**.

Aerodynamic and Weight Optimization

Reducing aerodynamic drag and overall weight also plays a crucial role in **increasing efficiency**. A streamlined design with **aerodynamic fairings** can reduce wind resistance, improving both range and top speed. Additionally, using **lightweight materials** such as **aluminum or carbon fiber** for the frame and battery casing can reduce the overall weight of the vehicle, allowing for better acceleration and longer range.

Regenerative Braking

Regenerative braking is an advanced feature that **recaptures energy lost during braking** and feeds it back into the battery. This system is commonly found in **electric cars, hybrid vehicles, and high-performance e-bikes**. Implementing regenerative braking in an electric two-wheeler requires a **compatible motor controller, proper wiring, and optimized settings**.

How Regenerative Braking Works

In a standard braking system, mechanical brakes convert kinetic energy into heat through friction, which **wastes energy**. Regenerative braking, however, allows the **electric motor to act as a generator**, converting kinetic energy back into electrical energy, which is then stored in the battery.

Types of Regenerative Braking Systems

There are two primary methods of regenerative braking:

1. **Passive Regenerative Braking:** This system automatically engages **when the throttle is**

released, using the motor's resistance to slow down the vehicle and recharge the battery.

2. **Active Regenerative Braking:** This method **activates when the brake lever is pulled**, sending a signal to the motor controller to convert braking force into electricity.

Implementing Regenerative Braking

To add regenerative braking, a **controller that supports regeneration** is required. Many **sine wave and vector controllers** come with built-in regenerative braking functionality. A **brake lever with an electrical switch** is needed to trigger the system when braking.

Component	**Function in Regenerative Braking**
Motor Controller	Regulates braking energy conversion
Throttle and Brake Sensors	Controls when regeneration occurs
Battery Pack & BMS	Stores recovered energy safely

Regenerative braking can typically **recover 5-15% of energy**, depending on riding conditions, terrain, and braking patterns. While it cannot fully replace mechanical brakes, it helps **extend range and reduce brake pad wear**.

Tuning Regenerative Braking

Many controllers allow customization of regenerative braking settings. If braking force is set too high, the vehicle may experience **sudden jerks** when braking, which can reduce ride comfort. A moderate setting ensures **smooth deceleration** while effectively recharging the battery.

Customizing an electric two-wheeler is a **continuous process** that allows riders to tailor their vehicle for **better range, speed, and efficiency**. **Upgrading batteries, motors, and controllers** can significantly improve performance, while **implementing regenerative braking** adds an energy recovery system that extends the ride distance.

For those looking to push the boundaries further, **aerodynamic modifications, smart displays, and advanced suspension upgrades** can further refine the riding experience.

Chapter 12

Smart Features & Aesthetic Upgrades

The evolution of electric two-wheelers is not just about **performance and efficiency**; modern advancements have introduced **smart features and aesthetic upgrades** that can enhance both **functionality and personalization**. Integrating **IoT (Internet of Things) technology, GPS tracking, and smartphone applications** into an electric two-wheeler can **redefine the riding experience** by providing **real-time monitoring, remote access, and enhanced security**. Additionally, **custom bodywork, paint jobs, and lighting modifications** allow riders to give their vehicles a **unique visual appeal** while improving visibility and safety.

This chapter explores the **technological and aesthetic enhancements** that can elevate an electric two-wheeler beyond a basic transportation tool, making it a **modern, high-tech, and personalized ride**.

Smart Features

Smart technology is **revolutionizing electric mobility**, allowing two-wheelers to be **connected, interactive, and more secure**. By integrating **IoT-enabled sensors, cloud connectivity, and smartphone apps**, riders can **track vehicle health, locate their bike remotely, monitor battery status,**

and even diagnose faults before they become major issues.

Integrating IoT for Smart Monitoring and Control

IoT integration involves **embedding sensors and connectivity modules** in the two-wheeler, allowing it to **communicate with smartphones and cloud servers**. A **GPS tracker, accelerometer, and onboard diagnostics module (OBD)** work together to **analyze riding behavior, detect faults, and provide real-time updates**.

A **smart controller** linked to an IoT platform enables **remote vehicle access**, allowing users to **lock/unlock the bike, track battery performance, adjust power settings, and even receive notifications** if unauthorized movement is detected.

Smart Feature	**Function**	**Benefit**
GPS Tracking	Real-time location tracking	Anti-theft security, trip logging
Smart BMS (Battery Management System)	Monitors charge cycles, voltage, temperature	Prevents battery damage, improves longevity
Remote	Uses Bluetooth or	Enhanced security

Smart Feature	Function	Benefit
Lock/Unlock	cellular network	and theft prevention
Ride Analytics	Tracks speed, energy usage, efficiency	Helps optimize range and performance
Geofencing	Creates a virtual boundary	Alerts user if the vehicle moves out of a designated area

A **cellular-enabled IoT module** can be installed within the **controller or battery pack**, connecting to a cloud platform where **riders can access real-time data through an app**. Some high-end electric motorcycles already feature **Wi-Fi and LTE connectivity**, but even **DIY builders** can integrate these features using **open-source IoT kits like ESP8266 or Raspberry Pi-based solutions**.

GPS Tracking for Security and Navigation

A **GPS tracker** is one of the most valuable smart features, providing **real-time location updates** and allowing the owner to **track their two-wheeler in case of theft**. Advanced GPS systems can be linked to **motion sensors** that send alerts if **unauthorized movement is detected**. Some GPS trackers also come with **emergency SOS features**, allowing riders to **send**

their location to emergency contacts in case of an accident.

Smartphone Apps for Monitoring and Control

Custom smartphone apps can be developed to **connect with the electric two-wheeler via Bluetooth, Wi-Fi, or LTE networks**. Through the app, riders can access **battery health, trip statistics, motor performance, and GPS data**. Some apps allow **controller tuning**, enabling users to **adjust acceleration, regenerative braking strength, and power modes**.

The table below compares different connectivity technologies used in smart electric two-wheelers:

Connectivity Type	**Range**	**Use Case**	**Pros**	**Cons**
Bluetooth	10-50m	Short-range control, local monitoring	Low power consumption, easy integration	Limited range
Wi-Fi	50-100m	Real-time updates when near	High data transfer speeds	Requires Wi-Fi access point

Connectivity Type	**Range**	**Use Case**	**Pros**	**Cons**
		Wi-Fi		
Cellular (4G/5G/LTE)	Global	Remote tracking, cloud-based analytics	Long-range coverage	Monthly subscription cost

A combination of **Bluetooth and cellular** connectivity is ideal, allowing **short-range local access** when near the vehicle and **remote access through cellular networks** when away.

Aesthetic Upgrades

Apart from functionality, a **well-designed electric two-wheeler should also reflect personal style and individuality**. Customizing the **bodywork, paint scheme, lighting, and visual elements** can enhance the **appearance, visibility, and uniqueness** of the vehicle.

Custom Bodywork for a Unique Look

Modifying the **frame, fairings, and panels** allows riders to create a **sleek, futuristic, or vintage** aesthetic based on their preference. Many DIY builders use **fiberglass, carbon fiber, or molded ABS plastic** to create **custom panels**.

Bodywork Material	Weight	Durability	Customization	Cost
Aluminum	Light	High	Medium	$$
Carbon Fiber	Ultra-light	Very High	Difficult	$$$$
Fiberglass	Medium	High	High	$$
ABS Plastic	Light	Medium	Very High	$

Using a **3D printer** or **CNC machine**, hobbyists can design **custom fairings, seat covers, and side panels** for their electric two-wheeler.

Custom Paint and Vinyl Wraps

A **high-quality paint job** or **vinyl wrap** can transform an electric two-wheeler's appearance. Paint customization involves using **automotive-grade**

enamel or polyurethane paints, which provide **durability against weather and UV exposure**.

Vinyl wraps are an **easier and reversible** option that allows **frequent design changes**. Some riders prefer **matte, chrome, or carbon fiber finishes**, giving the vehicle a **premium look**.

Lighting Modifications for Visibility and Style

Adding **custom lighting** enhances both **safety and aesthetics**. LED strips, underglow lighting, and **programmable RGB lights** allow riders to create **unique color effects** while improving nighttime visibility.

The table below highlights different lighting modifications and their benefits:

Lighting Upgrade	**Function**	**Benefit**
LED Headlights	Bright, energy-efficient lighting	Improved visibility, low power consumption
RGB Underglow Lights	Customizable underbody glow	Aesthetic appeal, increased visibility
Turn Signal Sequential	Flowing indicator lights	Stylish and attention-grabbing

Lighting Upgrade	Function	Benefit
LEDs		
Brake Light Flashers	Flashes upon braking	Enhanced safety, better alert for vehicles behind

Many modern electric motorcycles now integrate **adaptive lighting systems**, which **adjust brightness based on ambient light conditions** and even **change color according to riding modes**. DIY builders can achieve similar results using **Arduino or Raspberry Pi-based LED controllers**.

Integrating **smart features** and **aesthetic upgrades** can **transform an electric two-wheeler into a technologically advanced, stylish, and personalized vehicle**. **IoT-based monitoring systems, GPS tracking, and smartphone apps** offer convenience, security, and real-time analytics, making the vehicle more interactive and efficient. **Custom bodywork, premium paint jobs, and modern LED lighting** add an artistic and personal touch while also improving visibility and safety.

By combining **cutting-edge technology with aesthetic appeal**, an electric two-wheeler can be **more**

than just a mode of transportation—it becomes an extension of the rider's personality and innovation.

Legal & Safety Considerations

Electric two-wheelers are transforming personal mobility by offering an eco-friendly, efficient, and cost-effective mode of transportation. However, before riding an electric two-wheeler on public roads, it is crucial to understand **legal requirements, safety regulations, and best practices for riding and maintaining the vehicle**. Compliance with **local laws** ensures that the vehicle is legally permitted for use, while **proper safety gear and fire precautions** protect both the rider and the vehicle from potential hazards.

This chapter delves into the **legal framework surrounding electric two-wheelers**, the **essential safety gear** required for protection, and the **fire and electrical safety measures** that must be followed to handle high-power battery systems securely.

Understanding Local Laws

Before an electric two-wheeler can be used on public roads, riders must comply with the **local traffic laws and regulations** governing electric vehicles. These regulations vary **from country to country and even between states or provinces**. Understanding these laws is essential to avoid legal complications, fines, or restrictions on vehicle usage.

One of the first legal aspects to consider is whether the electric two-wheeler falls under the category of **low-speed electric bicycles**, **mopeds**, or **motorcycles**. Different jurisdictions classify electric two-wheelers based on their **motor power, top speed, and operational mode**.

Classification	**Motor Power (Watts)**	**Top Speed (km/h or mph)**	**License Required**	**Registration Required**
E-Bicycle	Below 750W	Up to 25 km/h (15 mph)	No	No
Electric Moped	750W - 4000W	25-45 km/h (15-28 mph)	Yes	Yes
Electric Motorcycle	Above 4000W	Over 45 km/h (28	Yes (Motorcycle License)	Yes

Classification	Motor Power (Watts)	Top Speed (km/h or mph)	License Required	Registration Required
		mph)		

Some **low-power electric bikes** (usually below 750W and under 25 km/h) may be classified similarly to bicycles and **do not require a license or registration**. However, more powerful electric scooters and motorcycles generally require a **driver's license, road registration, and insurance**.

Additionally, many countries have **helmet laws, lighting requirements, and insurance policies** that must be followed. Some **municipalities may restrict electric two-wheelers from riding on pedestrian pathways** or require them to use dedicated **bike lanes**.

Key Legal Aspects to Consider

License & Registration – Riders should check if their vehicle needs a motorcycle or moped license and ensure it is registered with the local transport authority.

Insurance Requirements – Some regions require liability insurance for electric two-wheelers, especially if they exceed certain speed limits.

Road Usage & Speed Limits – There may be **speed restrictions** in certain areas, such as school zones or bike lanes.

Helmet & Safety Gear Laws – Many places have **mandatory helmet laws** to protect riders from head injuries.

Lighting & Indicator Compliance – Electric two-wheelers often need **working headlights, brake lights, turn signals, and reflectors** to comply with road safety regulations.

Understanding these laws before purchasing or assembling an electric two-wheeler ensures that the rider avoids **fines, penalties, or potential confiscation of the vehicle**.

Safety Gear & Best Practices

Beyond legal requirements, safety gear plays a **crucial role in preventing injuries** during an accident or fall. Even though electric two-wheelers are often used for **short commutes**, the risk of **road accidents and injuries** is still significant. Wearing **protective gear, maintaining situational awareness, and following best riding practices** can **greatly reduce the likelihood of injuries**.

Essential Safety Gear for Riders

Helmet: The most critical piece of protective gear, a helmet **protects against head trauma** in the event of an accident. A **full-face helmet** offers the most protection, while **open-face and half helmets** provide less coverage but are still better than riding without one.

Gloves: Electric two-wheelers can reach high speeds, and in case of a fall, **gloves prevent injuries to the hands**. They also improve **grip and control**, reducing hand fatigue.

Protective Jacket & Pants: Wearing a **reinforced riding jacket and pants with padding or Kevlar lining** can protect against **abrasions and impact injuries**.

Knee & Elbow Guards: For additional protection, riders can use **joint guards**, especially if riding at **higher speeds or in traffic**.

Reflective Gear: Visibility is crucial for road safety. Wearing **high-visibility jackets, reflective armbands, or installing reflective strips** on the two-wheeler increases **nighttime visibility**.

Best Riding Practices for Safety

Always follow traffic rules, including speed limits and lane discipline.

Be aware of surrounding vehicles and pedestrians to avoid sudden obstacles.

Brake early and smoothly instead of sudden stops, especially in wet or slippery conditions.

Maintain a safe following distance to avoid collisions.

Use proper lighting and signals, especially at night or in poor weather conditions.

Inspect the two-wheeler regularly, checking tire pressure, brakes, and battery health before every ride.

By combining the **right safety gear with responsible riding habits**, riders can **minimize the risk of injury and enjoy a safer commuting experience**.

Fire & Electrical Safety

Electric two-wheelers rely on **high-capacity lithium-ion batteries**, which, if mishandled, can **overheat, catch fire, or explode**. Ensuring **proper charging, storage, and maintenance** of the battery and electrical system is essential for preventing **fire hazards and electrical failures**.

Common Causes of Battery Fires

Overcharging & Fast Charging Abuse: Leaving the battery plugged in beyond **100% charge** or using **low-quality fast chargers** can cause **overheating** and **thermal runaway**.

Physical Damage to Battery Cells: Dropping, puncturing, or overloading the battery pack can lead to **internal short circuits**, causing fires or explosions.

Improper Wiring & Loose Connections: Loose or poorly connected wires can **generate sparks and electrical shorts**, increasing the risk of fire.

Exposure to Water & Moisture: While some electric two-wheelers have **IP-rated waterproof enclosures**, **exposure to rain or submerged conditions** can cause electrical failures.

Use of Low-Quality or Mismatched Components: Using **non-certified chargers, poor-quality connectors, or incompatible battery cells** increases the risk of **malfunctions and fire hazards**.

Measures for Battery & Electrical Safety

Safety Measure	Purpose
Use a Certified BMS (Battery Management System)	Prevents overcharging, balances cells, and ensures safe operation.
Charge in a Well-Ventilated Area	Reduces heat buildup and prevents gas accumulation.
Inspect Wires &	Ensures no loose terminals, frayed cables, or corroded

Safety Measure	Purpose
Connections Regularly	connectors.
Avoid Fast Charging Frequently	Extends battery lifespan and prevents overheating.
Keep the Battery Away from Flammable Objects	Reduces the risk of fire spreading in case of thermal failure.
Use Proper Fuses & Circuit Breakers	Protects against short circuits and power surges.

By **adopting these safety measures**, riders can ensure **long battery life, prevent electrical hazards, and minimize the risk of fire incidents**.

Legal compliance and safety precautions are **non-negotiable aspects of owning and riding an electric two-wheeler**. Understanding **local laws, licensing requirements, and road regulations** ensures that the vehicle can be legally used without restrictions. Wearing **essential safety gear, following best riding practices, and maintaining proper fire and electrical safety protocols** significantly enhances both **rider safety and vehicle longevity**.

Chapter 13

Conclusion & Future Innovations

Electric two-wheelers are not just a means of transportation; they represent a shift toward **sustainable mobility, technological innovation, and personal engineering creativity**. Over the course of this book, readers have gained **deep insights into designing, building, and optimizing an electric two-wheeler from scratch**. From understanding the fundamentals of **battery technology, motor selection, and controller programming** to **legal compliance, safety measures, and performance tuning**, this journey has covered all aspects necessary for constructing a **functional, efficient, and roadworthy electric vehicle**.

At this stage, the knowledge acquired should empower the reader to **experiment, innovate, and refine their DIY electric two-wheeler project**. However, this is just the beginning. The field of electric mobility is **constantly evolving**, and numerous opportunities exist for further exploration—whether in **enhancing performance, integrating smart technologies, or even commercializing electric vehicle concepts**. This chapter will summarize the key takeaways from the book while exploring the **future of electric mobility** and the **potential pathways for expanding a DIY project into something even bigger**.

Key Lessons from This Journey

Building an electric two-wheeler from scratch requires **a structured approach that integrates mechanical design, electrical engineering, and software integration**. Each chapter of this book has laid the foundation for understanding **how different components interact** to create a smooth, efficient, and reliable electric vehicle.

Design & Chassis Fabrication: The book introduced the importance of **concept design, weight distribution, and structural integrity**. Through sketches and CAD modeling, an optimized frame was developed to ensure stability and efficiency. Various materials and fabrication techniques—such as **welding, tube bending, and reinforcement**—were explored for constructing a durable chassis.

Motor & Battery Selection: Choosing the right motor involved analyzing **power ratings, torque characteristics, and efficiency trade-offs**. The differences between **hub motors and mid-drive motors** were examined to help readers make informed decisions. Similarly, the battery section emphasized the importance of **battery chemistry, voltage, capacity, and thermal management**, ensuring the vehicle operates safely and efficiently.

Electronics, Wiring, and Control Systems: A deep dive into motor controllers, throttle systems, and instrumentation highlighted **how electrical components are interconnected**. Wiring diagrams and circuit protection mechanisms, such as **fuses and Battery Management Systems (BMS),** ensured the electrical integrity of the two-wheeler. Smart enhancements, including **GPS tracking, IoT connectivity, and regenerative braking**, were explored for additional functionality.

Safety, Testing & Troubleshooting: Before road deployment, the vehicle underwent **performance testing, initial power-up checks, and error diagnostics**. Common troubleshooting techniques for **motor malfunctions, controller errors, and battery issues** were provided, ensuring that readers could **resolve technical problems confidently**.

Legal Compliance & Road Safety: A key aspect of making an electric two-wheeler roadworthy is understanding **licensing, registration, and traffic regulations**. The book detailed essential **safety gear, riding best practices, and fire prevention strategies**, equipping riders with **the necessary knowledge to operate their vehicle responsibly**.

By mastering these core principles, a builder is now **capable of developing a fully functional electric**

two-wheeler, ready for daily commuting, testing, or even modification.

Future Possibilities in Electric Mobility

The field of electric vehicles is rapidly advancing, driven by **technological breakthroughs, sustainability goals, and the push for smarter, autonomous transportation**. The **future of electric two-wheelers** extends beyond what has been covered in this book, with several key trends shaping the next generation of electric mobility.

Advancements in Battery Technology

Energy storage remains the **biggest limiting factor** in electric mobility, but innovations in battery technology are gradually solving these challenges. **Solid-state batteries, graphene-enhanced lithium-ion cells, and ultra-fast charging technologies** are set to revolutionize the way electric vehicles operate. These advancements will lead to:

- **Higher energy densities**, allowing electric two-wheelers to travel much longer distances on a single charge.
- **Ultra-fast charging**, reducing charging times to **a few minutes instead of hours**.
- **Safer, non-flammable battery chemistries**, minimizing fire risks and improving longevity.

For DIY builders, these developments mean that future electric two-wheeler projects can incorporate **lighter, more powerful, and faster-charging battery solutions**.

Artificial Intelligence & Smart Connectivity

The integration of **AI-powered motor controllers, predictive analytics, and IoT-based tracking systems** is reshaping electric vehicle performance. Future enhancements may include:

- **Self-learning throttle responses**, where AI optimizes acceleration based on a rider's behavior.
- **Real-time GPS & remote diagnostics**, allowing riders to monitor battery health, motor efficiency, and security alerts from a smartphone app.
- **Autonomous navigation & safety features**, such as automatic collision avoidance and lane assistance.

These innovations will make electric two-wheelers **safer, smarter, and more interactive**, opening new possibilities for customization and user experience.

Regenerative Energy & Sustainability

As the world shifts towards sustainable transportation, electric vehicles will **incorporate more regenerative and energy-efficient systems**. Future two-wheeler designs may feature:

- **Enhanced regenerative braking systems**, allowing the vehicle to recover and store **more energy during deceleration**.
- **Solar-powered electric two-wheelers**, integrating **solar panels into the frame or battery system** for on-the-go charging.
- **Hydrogen fuel-cell electric bikes**, which could provide **an alternative power source** beyond traditional lithium-ion batteries.

Taking Your DIY Project to the Next Level

After successfully building an electric two-wheeler, there are several exciting ways to **expand upon this achievement**. Whether it's for **personal use, business opportunities, or open-source collaboration**, the next step is to refine, improve, and share the project with a wider audience.

Personal Customization & Performance Upgrades

Builders can continue improving their projects by experimenting with:

- **Higher-performance motors & batteries**, increasing speed, torque, and range.
- **Lightweight materials**, such as **carbon fiber frames**, for better efficiency.
- **Aerodynamic enhancements**, optimizing wind resistance to improve mileage.

Customizing an electric two-wheeler to **match personal commuting needs or off-road capabilities** can transform the project into a **unique, high-performance machine**.

Business & Commercialization Opportunities

Electric mobility is a booming industry, and those with **technical expertise in DIY electric vehicle construction** can explore business opportunities such as:

- **Developing conversion kits**, allowing others to upgrade bicycles and scooters into electric vehicles.
- **Building & selling custom electric two-wheelers**, creating a niche brand in the EV space.
- **Offering repair & upgrade services**, helping others maintain and enhance their EVs.

Turning a DIY passion into **a sustainable business** could provide long-term financial rewards while contributing to the green energy movement.

Open-Source Collaboration & Knowledge Sharing

For those who wish to **share their expertise with the global DIY community**, open-source collaboration is an excellent pathway. By **publishing designs, schematics, and build guides online**, individuals can:

- **Help others replicate and improve upon their designs**.
- **Receive community feedback**, leading to faster innovations and refinements.
- **Participate in global electric vehicle hackathons and competitions**.

Contributing to **forums, GitHub repositories, and open-source EV platforms** can **connect like-minded innovators and advance the DIY electric vehicle industry**.

The journey of building an electric two-wheeler **combines engineering, innovation, and sustainability**, proving that **individuals can create powerful, efficient transportation solutions without relying on large manufacturers**. The knowledge gained through this book serves as a **foundation for future exploration and creativity**, whether in refining personal projects, launching a business, or contributing to open-source innovation.

As technology continues to evolve, so do the possibilities for electric mobility. The future belongs to those who **experiment, learn, and push the boundaries of what's possible**. Whether it's **designing next-generation EVs, integrating AI-powered systems, or exploring alternative energy sources**, the DIY electric vehicle community has an exciting road ahead.

THE END

Made in the USA
Columbia, SC
11 June 2025

59305688R00093